LITERATURE OF SATIRE IN THE TWELFTH CENTURY

A Neglected Mediaeval Genre

LITERATURE OF SATIRE IN THE TWELFTH CENTURY

A Neglected Mediaeval Genre

Ronald E. Pepin

Studies in Mediaeval Literature
Volume 2

The Edwin Mellen Press
Lewiston/Queenston
Lampeter

Library of Congress Cataloging-in-Publication Data

Pepin, Ronald E.
  Literature of satire in the twelfth century.

  (Studies in mediaeval literature ; v. 2)
  Bibliography: p.
  Includes index.
  1. Verse satire, Latin (Medieval and modern)--
History and criticism. 2. Civilization, Medieval--
12th century. 3. Twelfth century. I. Title.
II. Series.
PA8060.P4 1988   871'.03'09   88-8469
ISBN 0-88946-316-6

> This is volume 2 in the continuing series
> Studies in Mediaeval Literature
> Volume 2 ISBN 0-88946-316-6
> SML Series ISBN 0-88946-314-X

Copyright © 1988 by Ronald E. Pepin

All rights reserved. For information contact:

The Edwin Mellen Press

Box 450   Box 67
Lewiston, New York   Queenston, Ontario
USA 14092   L0S 1L0 CANADA

Mellen House
Lampeter, Dyfed, Wales
UNITED KINGDOM SA48 7DY

Printed in the United States of America

Dedicated to

RITA EVA PEPIN

in appreciation of
her wonderful sense of
humor

CONTENTS

Preface ix
Chapter I: Twelfth Century Satire 1
Chapter II: Bernard of Morval 31
Chapter III: Hugh of Orleans 65
Chapter IV: Walter of Chatillon 89
Chapter V: Nigel of Canterbury 117
General Bibliography 161
Index 163

PREFACE

Recent anthologies of satirical literature leave a reader with the impression that formal satire faded with Juvenal, or Apuleius, and reappeared with Erasmus. This neglect of the entire medieval period ironically omits the most prolific era for Latin verse satire in literary history. The twelfth century witnessed an extraordinary outpouring of satiric genres, owing largely to the celebrated classical "renaissance." Throughout the 1100's, authors of first rank emerged in the cloister, court and school to ridicule the folly of men and institutions. Their poems are clever, their themes universal, their humor engaging -- in short, these writers are important contributors to the world's satiric literature.

This monograph presents an overview of Latin satire in the twelfth century and offers a closer analysis of four practitioners of the genre, two monks and two secular clerks, who represent the best of the age. Each wrote in Latin verses, following classical exemplars, scoring the vices and petty foibles of his times with exceptional vigor and wit. I hope the book will contribute to an increased knowledge of and appreciation for Bernard of Morval, Hugh of Orleans, Walter of Chatillon, Nigel of Canterbury, and Latin satire in the twelfth century. Since there are few published studies of these writers, especially the monks (Bernard and Nigel), I have included representative selections from the work of each, with my own literal translations into English.

My research into this subject has been supported by the National Endowment for Humanities through participation in four summer seminars for college teachers, at Dartmouth College (1975), the University of Pennsylvania (1978), Harvard University (1981), and Cornell University (1986). For numerous insights and much encouragement, I thank my colleagues in those seminars, and the directors: Stephen G. Nichols, Jr., Siegfried Wenzel, John Murdoch, and Robert Kaske.

LITERATURE OF SATIRE IN THE TWELFTH CENTURY

A Neglected Mediaeval Genre

CHAPTER I

TWELFTH CENTURY SATIRE

In the twelfth century, a classical revival occurred, fostered chiefly in the burgeoning schools and library centers of Europe. Sixty years ago, this "renaissance" was described in a pioneering study by Charles Homer Haskins.[1] Since then, the influence of this movement on the cultural life of the times, and particularly on the various academic disciplines, has been amply investigated and documented.[2] Certainly this is true of History, Rhetoric, Jurisprudence and, in general, Literature. Satire, too, shared in this momentous revival.

Numerous factors contributed to the re-emergence of Latin verse satire on a large scale in the twelfth century.[3] The dramatic increase in the number of schools from 1100 on accounts largely for the phenomenon. The rapid development and expansion of cathedral schools, with their emphasis on Latin grammar and imitative exercises, exposed their pupils to Roman satire as well as to the epics of Vergil and Lucan. The students were receptive to the ironic wit, sardonic exclamation and bold obscenity of the Roman masters. An increasing student community, with its attendant impatience and discontent, naturally accompanied the growth of the schools.[4] In addition, the cloistered scholae and libraries, older establishments which continued to flourish in the twelfth century, provided monastic writers with access to the classics, including satirists. There is overwhelming evidence that the monks absorbed the satiric spirit and practiced its forms.

The schools and the literate class they produced do not solely account for the satiric outpouring of the twelfth century. Conditions in society invited the cynical responses which a learned group was able to express with biting wit and polished verse. Abuses in the Church, especially those deriving from fiscal administration after the Gregorian reforms, sparked an unprecedented outburst of satirical protest. Educational innovations, notably the increasing prominence of logic, vocationalism, and the concomitant decline of the traditional arts curriculum, provoked numerous satires decrying the misdirection of schools and masters. Also, institutions of secular government, including the morals and manners of courtiers, became objects of severe reproach as the century progressed. These satires were often compositions of disappointed men whose clerical training did not secure them rewarding employment, or those unhappily dependent on patronage.[5] Before considering the major themes in greater detail, let us recall the Roman exemplars who directly shaped the satiric impulse of the age.

Quintilian claimed satire as an invented genre of his nation.[6] Certainly, Ennius, Lucilius and their literary descendants created a distinctive and highly influential body of writing broadly defined as a continuous piece of verse, or prose mingled with verse . . . generally characterized by the free use of conversational language, the frequent intrusion of its author's personality, its predilection for wit, humour, and irony, great vividness and concreteness of description, shocking obscenity in theme and language, an improvisatory tone, topical subjects, and the general intention of improving society by exposing its vices and follies.[7]

The outstanding Roman satirists were Horace (65-8 B.C.), Persius (34-62) and Juvenal (50-ca.127), from whom the twelfth century writers borrowed liberally. They appropriated proper names, motifs, expressions, entire passages. They departed from the masters in form, however, often abandoning the hexameter, the traditional measure of Roman satirists. Moreover, the twelfth-century writers drew as freely on ironic and humorous sources which would not be grouped technically within the genre, such as Ovid's Ars Amatoria and Remedia Amoris, Martial's epigrams, and the comedies of Terence. Yet, the uses of Seneca's Apocolocyntosis and Petronius' Cena Trimalchionis were rare.[8]

The frequency of citations from and allusions to Horace, Persius and Juvenal among the satirists of the twelfth century establishes that they were curriculum authors of wide appeal. Certain phrases and whole lines from their poems recur so often as to be conventional and proverbial. Some of their themes, e.g., Juvenal's bitter portrait of senectitude or his vehement misogyny, became commonplaces. Genial Horace, stoic Persius, and strident Juvenal all found imitators.[9] Furthermore, the classical satirists were subjects of numerous commentaries which presented them as eloquent reprovers of vice, as moralists addressing not only ancient Rome, but all times. Surely this is why John of Salisbury designated Horace and Juvenal as "ethici," moralists.[10] They were the supreme exemplars of a genre for which the age was crying out, and in poems of twelfth-century imitators, they continued to mock folly and depravity.

The <u>sermones</u> of Horace and the <u>satirae</u> of Juvenal were complemented as satirical sources by Christian liturgy and Sacred Scripture, which were irreverently plundered for scathing humor, especially parody. Scenes from the Gospels, sayings of the prophets, ceremonies of the liturgical year, even the Evangelists' names (e.g., <u>Luca</u> = <u>lucrum</u>) were distorted to serve the ends of satire, especially criticism of avarice and simony.[11] The most sharp-tongued of the Patristic writers, Saint Jerome, provided the learned clerics of the 1100's with Christian prose of undeniably satirical character.[12] Abundant sources, clearly, were available to the men of the schools whose indignation was aroused and whose avenues of recourse were largely blocked. One path ever-open to the witty erudite is satire, and among circles of learned friends, in schools, courts and cloisters, an unparalleled satiric explosion occurred in twelfth-century Europe.

The "beneficent poison of satire" was administered so liberally in this period that no secular or ecclesiastical institution escaped scrutiny, no vice went unexposed, no class unscathed.[13] Of course, the gravity and extent of some abuses prompted such a satirical outpouring as to become major objects of ridicule.

The school-trained clerics and learned monks who composed the satires of the twelfth century quite naturally assailed abuses in the Church and cloister most vigorously and frequently. Their poems constantly mocked a slothful clergy neglectful of spiritual duties and given entirely to gluttony, lust and the pursuit of material goods. Throughout the century, they endlessly censured avarice and venality in the chanceries, especially in the Roman Curia.[14] These themes are addressed often in the Carmina Burana of the celebrated Benediktbeuern manuscript, which also includes a version of the famous "Gospel According to Mark Silver."[15] The satirists relentlessly attacked the selling and buying of sacred offices, the sins of Giezi and Simon Magus, who are named often in their poems.

One distressing abuse which the satirists mocked unreservedly was the ordination and consecration of children in holy orders. Scripture, in I Timothy (ch. 3) had proscribed the admission of neophytes (i.e., the newly-baptized) to bishoprics. Relying on this authority, the satirists ridiculed the growing practice of the consecration of "boy-bishops." For example, Bernard of Morval (De contemptu mundi III. 391 ff.) heaped invective on this turba neophyta; Nigel of Canterbury (Speculum Stultorum 2749 ff.) brilliantly lampooned Robekinus ("Little Robby") holding the keys to the church while still wailing in his cradle. The Lateran Council of 1179 finally attempted to prevent this scandal which the satirists had decried for most of the century.

Worldly excesses among the spiritual leaders of the Church, especially avarice, sloth, gluttony and lust, were constant targets of satirical barbs. The twelfth-century poets created the caricature of the slovenly bishop, stuffed with fat capons, carried in a drunken stupor to his soft bed, attended by fawning retainers and lusty wenches, deaf to the poor crying at his gate. Of course, this mercenary prelate, no shepherd to his flock, plunders the goods of his people, or abandons them to other wolves, while he goes hunting. Such is the portrait of the luxurious bishop drawn in the pointedly detailed verses of Bernard of Morval and Nigel of Canterbury. Both writers mocked the penchant for hunting among the higher clergy long before Chaucer would ironically satirize the vice in his portly monk "that lovede venerie."

If the corruption and ignorance of the higher clergy, the greed of the Roman Curia, and scandalous simony constituted major themes of satire, no less did the vices of monks escape its attention. Monastic foundations were ridiculed for their luxury, while monks themselves were mocked for breach of their vows of poverty, chastity, obedience and stability. From within and without, the cloister was the target of bitter invective and sharp derision for its hypocrisies, its abandonment of the founders' purposes. In such pieces as "Ordo monasticus" by Wilchard of Lyon, written in hexameters, and "De vita monachorum" by Roger, a monk of Bec, a litany of shameful monastic abuses was proclaimed.[16] Many clerics and monks exercised their barbed wit on the abbots, priors and brothers whose rampant vices could not be concealed beneath habits and cowls.

Not only were the individual vices of monks roundly satirized, but so were the religious orders and foundations themselves. Anglo-Latin authors of the twelfth century were especially outspoken in their critical reviews of the proliferating monastic orders.[17] John of Salisbury, a writer with a distinctly-satirical disposition, and his younger contemporary, Gerald of Wales, both included cynical descriptions of numerous orders in their prose compositions.[18] Walter Map, the outstanding prose satirist of the age, did likewise in De nugis curialium, devoting considerable space to the various orders, and one long chapter on monks in general, opening with the statement,

> Monks, both white and black, recognize their prey, as the hawk spies the frightened lark . . .
>
> (Monachi tam albi quam nigri, sicut nisus alaudam territam, ita predam suam agnoscunt)[19]

He reserved his sharpest censure for Cistercians, accusing them of manifold crimes, not even sparing Bernard of Clairvaux in his ridicule. Map, who often credited himself with clever retorts and witty sayings, reported a conversation between two Cistercian abbots in the company of Bishop Gilbert Foliot of London about the miracles of Saint Bernard. One told of how the miraculous ability sometimes failed even the great Bernard, as when he lay once upon a dead boy, but was unable to restore him to life. At this admission, Map, who was present, declared:

> He was most unfortunate of monks, for I have never heard that any monk lay upon a boy, but that the boy immediately afterward stood erect (Ch. 1.24).

(Monachorum infelicissimus hic fuit. Nunquam enim audivi quod aliquis monachus super puerum incubuisset quin statim post ipsum surrexit puer.)

Nigel of Canterbury also has an extensive review of orders in Speculum Stultorum. All these writers marshaled before the reader white monks (Cistercians) and black (Cluniacs), Praemonstratensians and Carthusians, Hospitallers and Templars, and a host more, indicted for rapacity, debauchery and grand offenses, as well as ridiculed for petty evasions of their own rules. The forms of these invectives were a clever blend of valid praise and wry insinuation of hypocrisy and vice. For example, rules of silence, abstention from meat, and other ascetic rigors were introduced as ideals, and then, through innuendo and explicit examples alike, the satirists illustrated monastic practices which made a mockery of the rule. Often, a particular canon gave rise to pointed jests, as in the frequent ribaldry directed at the Cistercians for their prohibition against wearing breeches beneath the habit.

The clerical satirists at times directed witty criticism at the schools themselves. From its first decades, the twelfth century witnessed a "bataille des arts," as one vernacular poem of the next century called it.[20] A fundamental conflict developed between the claims of "new" logic and the traditional curriculum authors (auctores). Humanistic studies gradually gave way to utilitarian specialization, and grammar (the classics) yielded more and more to "logic-chopping" (professional disputation).[21] The most outspoken critic of these tendencies was John of Salisbury, who devoted a prose treatise, Metalogicon (1159), to the defense of broad classical education and the verbal arts. He assailed the sect of "Cornificius," which maintained that eloquence was a natural gift requiring no special studies for its cultivation, but practice only.[22] "Cornificius" and his disciples abandoned grammar and logic in its broadest sense as fruitless, a waste of time. In his verse <u>Entheticus</u>, John satirized the same outlook in the school of "Sertorius," whom he accused of teaching his young disciples, for a great fee, to know nothing! John mocked the intellectual immaturity and shallowness of this school at length, focusing especially on its neglect of the authors:

>Thus, unless you speak in language suited to children,
>This chattering crowd will spit in your face.
>If you know the authors, if you review ancient writings
>To establish a precedent for your case,
>They all cry out, 'where is this old ass headed?
>Why relate words and deeds of the ancients to us?
>We are wise of ourselves, our youth has taught itself,
>Our troop has no need of ancient teachings.
>We do not accept the burden of pursuing lessons of those
>Whom Greece and Rome honor as authors!

>(Sic nisi complacito pueris sermone loquaris,
>   Conspuet in faciem garrula turba tuam.
>Si sapis auctores, veterum si scripta recenses,
>   Ut statuas, si quid forte probare velis,
>Undique clamabunt 'vetus hic quo tendit asellus?
>   Cur veterum nobis dicta vel acta refert?
>A nobis sapimus, docuit se nostra juventus,

> Non recipit veterum dogmata nostra cohors,
> Non onus accipimus, ut eorum verba sequamur,
> Quos habet auctores Graecia, Roma colit.)[23]

Another object of satire was the courtier class. A considerable body of anti-court satire was composed from mid-century on, mocking the trifling pursuits of courtiers at one end of the scale, and their vicious crimes at the other. In this theme also, Anglo-Latin writers took the lead. John of Salisbury's Entheticus vehemently ridiculed the court of "Hircanus" (a name derived from hircus, "goat," surely suggesting wantonness, but probably also punning on Henricus, "Henry"). The poet unsparingly derides a drunken court (ebria curia) under a "boy-king," and he exposes the decadent life of courtiers (aulici) who love vices and despise virtues.[24] Nigel of Canterbury reserved a portion of Speculum Stultorum for the same theme, and he also wrote a bold treatise on the subject, prefaced by a satirical prologue in elegiac verses.[25]

The Architrenius ("Arch-Mourner") of John de Hauville, a poet with distinct ties to England, also addressed the theme of courtly corruption. This long, difficult, "lugubrious Latin poem of some merit," relates the journey of a youth who laments his dissolute life and seeks Natura's assistance in combatting his slothful and vicious propensities.[26] His search for the goddess leads him to real places, e.g., Paris, and, more often, to symbolic abodes, such as the House of Venus and the Hill of Presumption. The fourth book of this involved allegory finds him at the Mount of Ambition, where he reviews the luxurious decadence of courtiers who reside there. After describing a lavish scene, he turns to the familiar complaints about the court:

At court there is no trust, no respect, no moderation
In crime. The court is addicted to vices, oppresses integrity
With ambition, inclines toward every source of gain;
Wherever it strives with zeal to increase its purse,
It sells the assent of the tongue for a price;
Courtiers seize the greater bribes of patrons,
And sometimes a mark of favor is shared by adversaries.
He who promises one allegiance to both parties
Aids neither, and bound to each, betrays both.
For a soldier either refuses arms to each,
Or protecting each, he threatens both.

(Nulla fides aule, nulla est reverencia, nullus
Committendo modus. Viciis indulget, honestum
Ambicione premit, equum declinat in omni
Materia lucri, studio quocunque laborat,
Ut loculus crescat, linque suffragia vendit
Ad precii libram, rapiunt maiora patronum
Munera nec numquam partitur puncta favoris
Partibus adversis, unum promittit utrimque
Obsequium, neutrumque iuvat, qui utrique tenetur,
Proditor amborum; nam vel bellator utrimque
Arma negat, vel utrique favens utrique minatur.)

(IV.338-48)

By the end of the century, Walter Map was comparing the court to Hell. Though he concluded that the royal court was not exactly Hell, yet it lacked none of the torments associated with the infernal realms. The thirst of Tantalus is paralleled by the thirst for the goods of others, the restlessness of Sisyphus matched by the covetousness of the courtiers (curiales), and so on. Map's digressive treasury of archaic lore, anecdotes and exempla begins with and ends with the court, which the satirist proclaims to be a place of punishment as similar to Hell as a horse's shoe to a mare's.[27]

The literary history of misogyny and misogamy extends from Man's most ancient texts to modern times. In the Western tradition, from Semonides' comparison of wives to animals, saving praise for only the woman whose industry is like the bee, and the bitter railings of Juvenal, who declared a good woman to be as rare as a black swan, women and marriage have been objects of satirical invective. Moreover, the religious zeal and sharp wit of certain Church Fathers, notably Tertullian and Jerome, combined to perpetuate and legitimize antifeminist outpourings. This is so commonly known and well documented that one need not trace again its glum development.[28] However, an important point to make is that misogyny was so commonplace among the auctores of satire as to become an established convention in the twelfth century. Juvenal was a popular school model, while the reading of educated monks and clerics alike included Jerome's important treatises. The former's infamous sixth satire, and the latter's Adversus Jovinianum, with its abundant classical examples of misogamy, invariably occur, through citation, verbal echoes or allusions, in the antifeminist texts of the twelfth century. Therefore, the satirist of this period followed this convention as a display of erudition, and an exercise in skillful imitation. This is not to deny that many writers of the era, especially monks, found the themes congenial and their expression useful to support the ideals of chastity and celibacy.

Monks were not the sole composers of misogynistic invective, although theirs is the most vehement and sustained. In the first year of the twelfth century, or close to it, a canon of Saint Omer named Petrus Pictor wrote verses which found many imitators. In a poem of eighty-six lines <u>De muliere mala</u>, he likened evil women to frightful perils, such as wild beasts and consuming flames:

> A woman's ferocity exceeds all the world's wild beasts,
> She exceeds the plundering tiger and the enraged lion . . .
> Woman is a raging flame burning more fiercely than fire;
> She has terrified, she ignites, she has consumed the world.
>
> (Prestat in orbe feris cunctis feritas mulieris,
> Tygri predoni prestat rabidoque leoni . . .
> Femina flamma furens, sed flammis acrius urens,
> Totum concussit mundum, succendit et ussit.)[29]

He went on to blame the wicked woman for confusion on earth and the death of souls. Following Saint Jerome, Pictor enumerated the men of old who were ruined by women, naming directly or alluding to Joseph, Samson, Solomon, John the Baptist, and more. His examples were not confined to Scripture, for he laments the fate of Hippolytus, Amphiaraus, Cynyras and Nisus, among others.

In the first quarter of the century, Marbod of Rennes and Hildebert of Lavardin, bishops, composed verses similar to those of Petrus Pictor, and to each other.[30] Both employed violent images of women's destructive power; both assembled catalogues of victims destroyed by women's wiles. Their poems, in turn, influenced the author of the most protracted satire of mala femina in the century, Bernard of Morval, whose work I shall analyze more closely in a later chapter.

The satires of women by Petrus Pictor, Marbod and Hildebert vie with one another in outrageous vocabulary. Women are compared to frightful beasts (wolves and lions), loathsome creatures (night owls and serpents), deadly perils (fire and poison). The paradox of their fatal charms is emphasized in such terms as dulce malum ("sweet evil") and pulchra putredo ("lovely rottenness"). Often, through double entendre, the synonyms for women are obscene: deep ditch, slippery way, common entrance. The poets never tire of anaphora, as illustrated in these lines of Marbod:

> Who urged our first parent to taste forbidden fruit?
> Woman. Who made daughters corrupt their father?
> Woman. Who ruined a brave man robbed of his hair?
> Woman. Who cut off the sacred head of a just man?
> Woman. . . .
>
> (Quis suasit primo vetitum gustare parenti?
> Femina. Quis patrem natas vitiare coegit?
> Femina. Quis fortem spoliatum crine peremit?
> Femina. Quis justi sacrum caput ense recidit?
> Femina. . . .)
>
> (PL 171, col. 1698)

Alliteration abounds in their poems, especially of " f." _Femina_ is modified by _foetida_ (foul), _fervida_ (burning), _fragilis_ (fragile); identified with _fossa_ (ditch), _favus_ (honeycomb), _fax_ (torch), _flamma_ (flame), _fovea_ (pit), _furor_ (madness); linked to _fallere_ (to deceive), _frangere_ (to break), _fingere_ (to invent). Clearly, these poets are upholding satire's traditional hyperbole, obscenity and shocking wordplay. Such an exercise may seem warped and cruel to us, but I trust that the satirists who wrote and read these verses found them inventive, clever, and humorous.

Another constant, long-lived device of antifeminist satire was the citation of classical and Scriptural precedents, sometimes mingled, in catalogue form. As we have seen, Petrus Pictor assembled an extensive list of ancient victims. His formula was followed closely by other writers who accused women of the confounding of David and Solomon, the imprisonment of Joseph, the blinding of Samson and the beheading of John the Baptist. Here Hildebert of Lavardin may serve as a typical, brief example:

> A woman robbed Paris of his wits, Uriah of his life,
> David of his loyalty and Solomon of faith.
> A woman was enough to condemn John to death,
> Hippolytus to ruin, Joseph to chains.

> (Femina mente Parim, vita spoliavit Uriam,
>   et pietate David, et Salomona fide.
> Femina sustinuit iugulo damnare Ioannem,
>   Ypolitum lethe, compedibusque Ioseph.)
>   (Scott #50.23-26)

Such catalogues continue to appear in Latin verse satire throughout the twelfth century, and in its closing decades they occur with some frequency in more serious, didactic books, and in sermons as well.[31] One couplet of remarkable popularity and durability was Roger of Caen's rhetorical question:

> If Lot, Samson, David and Solomon
> A woman destroyed, who now will be safe?
>
> (Si Loth, Samsonem, si David, si Salomonem
>   Femina dejecit, quis modo tutus erit?)
>   (Wright, p. 188)

These lines, and the earlier satirical catalogues of destructive women and fallen men, became a legacy for writers whose genres were as varied as Provencal lyrics and Salimbene's Chronica. The misogynistic formulas were translated into French and English, appearing in lyrics, such as "The Nightingale and the Thrush," and in Sir Gawain and the Green Knight.[32] Clearly, the misogynistic conventions of Latin verse satire proved adaptable, and convenient, to other popular literary types.

Satire of marriage was more restricted in the twelfth century, owing undoubtedly to the fact that monastic writers, and most clerics, concerned themselves primarily with assailing the wiles of seductive women rather than an institution in which they had no part. However, a number of misogamistic satires remain, chiefly in the form of counsels against marriage. Such pieces usually contain a litany of marital woes, and inevitable appeals to authority. These elements are traceable to Jerome's Adversus Jovinianum, a work of immense appeal among twelfth-century writers, as noted above. As part of his attack on Jovinian's position that marriage could be a state as meritorious in Christian life as virginity, Jerome had marshaled authorities who derided married life. One work Jerome claims to rely on is a tract of Theophrastus entitled <u>Aureolus Liber de nuptiis</u> ("The Golden Book on Marriage") in which the question is posed, "should a wise man take a wife?". The answer, of course, is a resounding "no!," with an appended catalogue of horrors stemming from the very nature of women. The citation of this book, <u>Aureolus</u> (which probably never existed), along with Jerome's many examples attributed to it, and the name, Theophrastus, became commonplaces of misogamist literature.

The most famous and enduring satire on marriage in the century was <u>Dissuasio Valerii</u> by Walter Map. In the form of an epistle of "Valerius" (perhaps intended to call to mind Valerius Maximus, whose collection of memorable sayings and deeds was a popular sourcebook for medieval writers) to his friend "Rufinus," Map issued a wry warning against marriage. The letter borrows both material and tone from St. Jerome. It is replete with allusions and examples supporting the thesis that a wise man should never marry. While contrasting his own devotion to unadorned truth with Rufinus' deluded passion, the author weaves into his counsel all the topoi of earlier satires on this theme. He describes the downfall of Adam, David, Solomon and Samson; he turns to pagan gods and demigods humiliated by women, including Mars, Jupiter, Apollo and Hercules; he adds detailed anecdotes about the rulers and philosophers of ancient times who proved, in words and deeds, the folly of marriage. Map even ended the piece with the advice that its recipient read the <u>Aureolus</u> of Theophrastus and Ovid's <u>Medea</u>. Of course, a brief overview cannot do justice to Map's clever expression, his witty innuendo, his brilliant ordering of well-worn themes, but the lasting appeal of the Dissuasio Valerii confirms Map's ability to render the old new. The work, which circulated independently, was later incorporated by its author into the digressive miscellany of De nugis curialium. Soon, references to it as an authoritative source called "Valerius," often in company with "Theophrastus," began to appear in literature. One finds it, for example, in Richard de Bury's Philobiblon ("Liber Theophrasti aut Valerii") and Chaucer's prologue to the Wife of Bath's tale ("He cleped it Valerie and Theofraste").[33]

Though churchmen, schoolmasters, courtiers and women were major objects of satiric composition in the twelfth century, no class of society escaped ridicule entirely. A form which embraced whole populations developed, especially among Anglo-Latin writers.[34] Known as Satira communis, this type of invective reviewed the classes from kings to lowly peasants. A brief example is the poem appended by Henry of Huntingdon to his Historia Anglorum. In seventy-four hexameters, Henry outlines the failings of bishops, priests, monks and laymen.[35] A more comprehensive review of society occurs in Bernard of Morval's De contemptu mundi, where, in order, the poet satirizes bishop, king, priest, cleric, soldier, nobleman, magistrate, merchant and farmer. Each is summarily introduced in two lines, and then Bernard proceeds to specify his complaints about them in turn. The entire passage numbers over one hundred and twenty lines (II.239-362), though the treatment of each class is uneven, with the higher stations receiving more attention. Sometimes the satira communis is woven into another narrative, as Nigel of Canterbury does in Speculum

Stultorum, a work whose very title implies that many will behold themselves in the mirror of folly. Indeed, at one point Nigel moves his reader's attention from the Roman Curia to an extensive satiric inspection (lines 2495-2922) of kings, bishops, abbots and priors. Occasionally, the satirists isolated a particular group or class for special ridicule, as, for example, John of Salisbury's attack on treacherous hosts who lie in wait for unwary travelers. This satire occupies about one hundred lines (1530-1636) of his Entheticus.

The foregoing survey of twelfth-century satirical forms and themes is merely an introduction to a subject which awaits exhaustive treatment. A comprehensive history of satiric expression in this prolific era would elaborate on this material, and would include numerous other objects of ridicule, important figures, and collections of verse whose intention seems wholly, or in part satirical. Clearly, many of the "Goliardi" lyrics qualify as satire, as does the famous Metamorphosis Goliae.[36] The small collection of poems by the "Archpoet" is regarded by some as satirical in nature, though I place these clever appeals for patronage outside the purview of satire. One exception is the longer piece known as "The Archpoet's Confession," which contains a mock-warning of the dangers of love (Venus), gambling (ludus) and drinking (taberna).[37] In addition, the history of twelfth-century satire would surely address the satiric elements in other formal genres, notably homilies and epistles.

To confirm the satiric temper of preaching at this time, one need only read a few Latin sermons on the dangers of money or on the deadly sins at work in the world. He may review the themes, exempla and modes of address so richly documented in G. R.

Owst's book on English homily. In that work, for example, the author cites (page 385) as a homiletic commonplace the motif we have observed in Latin verse satire:

> Who was stronger than Samson, wiser than Solomon, holier than David? And yet they were all overthrown by woman's wiles.

Certain sermons display other satirical ornamentations, such as irony, puns, humorous anecdotes, even fables. Owst affirms that such preaching was a source of inspiration for poets of the century, which might be too sweeping a conclusion. Nevertheless, satirical elements were widely employed in Latin and vernacular sermons, and the reciprocal influence of verse satire and homily is undeniable.

Some collections of epistles also display satirical tendencies, often abundantly. In fact, lines from classical satirists are frequently discovered in the more urbane compositions of the humanist letter-writers, which are also noted for irony, anecdotes, and sharp humor. These features stand out especially in early epistles of John of Salisbury, and in some by his friend, Peter of Blois.[38] For example, the latter directed one of his letters (#79) to the commonplace theme of misogyny. The piece mockingly rehearses examples and anecdotes garnered from past authorities, including Juvenal, and Jerome's "Aurelius (sic) Theophrastus," all for the benefit of R. the deacon who has just entered the accursed state of matrimony. Another (#14) assails the ambition and vanity of clerics who neglect their real calling, the care of souls, to follow the disordered, hectic rounds of courtly life. Peter mocks their misplaced values by enumerating, in vivid detail, the vexations of courtiers, such as poor lodgings, horrid food and drink, sudden, early excursions at the king's whim. Alliteration, parallelism and other rhetorical devices accentuate Peter's hyperbolic humor in depicting the inconveniences of courtiers. For example, after describing the wine served to courtiers as spoiled by must and sourness, clouded, greasy, rancid, dark and flat, the author places himself at the scene:

> Sometimes I have seen wine served so thick with dregs that it had to be poured through a sieve rather than drunk, with eyes shut and teeth clenched, with trembling and mouth agape. The beer drunk at court is dreadful in taste, abominable in sight.
>
> (Vidi aliquando vinum adeo faeculentum magmatibus apponi, quod non nisi clausis oculis, et consertis dentibus, cum horrore et rictu, cribrari oportebat potius quam potari. Cerevisia, quae in curia, bibitur, horrenda gustu, abominabilis est aspectu.)
> (<u>PL</u> 207, col. 47)

Peter continues in this vein. The court is so crowded with people to be fed that animals are bought for food whether they are healthy or not; neither the rottenness nor the stench of four-day old fish reduces their price. Those who serve the meals are unconcerned about the death or sickness of the miserable guests, provided only that their masters' tables have ample portions. The courtiers are filled with carrion, and the bellies of those at the table become tombs for many corpses. Peter does not hesitate to assail types at court either. For instance, of the mareschalli, or horsekeepers, he writes:

> Indeed, these are the most fawning flatterers, the worst detractors, the most shameless cheaters. They are most churlish until they receive something. When they have received, they are ungrateful, and unless the giver continues to give, they are his enemies.
>
> (Hi siquidem blandissimi sunt adulatores, detractores pessimi, improbissimi emunctores. Importunissimi sunt, donec accipiant; cum acceperint, sunt ingrati; et nisi manum suam donator continuet, inimici.) (PL 207, col. 48)

Though Peter does not elaborate on all types that populate the court, he underscores its folly with a satirical list that includes stage-players, gamblers, flatterers, hucksters, mimes, rascals, barbers, buffoons, and the like.[39]

Monastic epistles (and treatises) often evidence not only an appreciation for wit and humor, but for satire, and they occasionally employ its chief devices of reproach and correction, namely irony and exaggeration. Saint Bernard satirized vices (vitia) of Cluniac monks in his Apology to Wm., Abbot of St. Theoderic. In this brilliantly-ironic piece, the author ridiculed excesses in the monks' habits of eating, drinking, sleeping, and in their extravagant clothing.[40] Peter the Venerable, a Cluniac abbot, was no less sparing of his brothers. In a letter to his priors, he addressed the monks in most unflattering terms which import a bitter satirical comparison to beasts and birds of prey:

> Listen, ravenous monk! You should not be angry that I name you so, for in what do you differ from a raven, in what from a vulture, in what from a bear, in what from a wolf? Those birds and beasts gape at bloody feasts, neither do they distinguish day from day nor hour from hour in feeding. So, as I see, do you also, who, as I have written above, allow no season, no day to be free from such eating, except when you are compelled by force.
>
> (Audi, corvine monache, nec irascaris quia te sic nomino. In quo enim differs a corvo, in quo a vulture, in quo ab urso, in quo a lupo? Inhiant volucres illae aut ferae sanguineis dapibus, nec dies a diebus nec horas ab horis in vescendo discernunt. Sic ut video et tu, qui (ut supra scripsi) nullum tempus, nullam diem, nisi quando vi cogeris, a tali esu vacare permittis.)[41]

The satiric impulse, then, manifested itself in numerous literary genres of the twelfth century. Prose compositions, such as treatises and epistles, as well as poetic efforts of various kinds exhibited the common tendency to satirize and reflected the influence of ancient forms. In subsequent chapters I shall examine the work of four men whose writings are notably diverse, though each is an outstanding example of satire. Two were secular clerks, two monks. Hugh of Orleans composed lyrics whose wonderful vitality and pointed wit exemplify the satirical instinct in the "wandering scholars" of the age. Walter of Chatillon, a schoolmaster who interrupted his academic career for royal service, invented rhythmic forms to score abuses in schools, church and state. Bernard of Morval, a Cluniac monk, chastized the malice and folly of contemporary society in a long work which one respected scholar classifies a "complaint," not a satire. Nigel of Canterbury, monk of Christchurch, has left a truly satirical medley of enduring appeal in his rambling fable of Burnellus the ass. All of these men were skillful Latin poets. All exposed to ridicule the foolishness and vice of their society. All have enriched the world's literature. Whether they affected contemporary morality or not is unknown, but they have surely endowed the modern reader with an insightful, if grimaced depiction of human activity in a momentous age.

CHAPTER ONE

NOTES

[1] Charles H. Haskins, The Renaissance of the Twelfth Century (Cambridge, Ma., 1927).

[2] In 1977, a conference marking the fiftieth anniversary of Haskins' book was held in Cambridge. Twenty-six scholarly papers presented at that meeting were published under the title, Renaissance and Renewal in the Twelfth Century, eds. R. L. Benson and G. Constable, with Carol D. Lanham (Cambridge, Ma., 1982).

[3] A brief, but useful essay on the subject is Rodney M. Thomson, "The Origins of Latin Satire in Twelfth Century Europe," Mittellateinisches Jahrbuch 13 (1977) 73-83.

[4] Thomson, 79.

[5] Peter Dronke, "Profane Elements in Literature," in Renaissance and Renewal, 583.

[6] G. L. Hendrickson, "Satura Tota Nostra Est," Classical Philology XXII (January, 1927) 46-60.

[7] Gilbert Highet, The Classical Tradition (Oxford, 1967 repr.) 305. Highet's major contribution to the study of the genre is The Anatomy of Satire (Princeton, N.J., 1962).

[8] The rarity of Petronius manuscripts is discussed by Janet Martin, "Uses of Tradition: Gellius, Petronius, and John of Salisbury," Viator 10 (1979) 57-76.

[9] Horace was "the most popular of the three," according to Thomson, 77. Gilbert Highet has a small chapter on "Juvenal in Medieval Culture," in Juvenal the Satirist (Oxford, 1954).

[10] Ronald E. Pepin, "John of Salisbury's Entheticus and the Classical Tradition of Satire," Florilegium 3 (1981) 215-27. On commentaries, see B. Bischoff, "Living with the Satirists," in Classical Influences on European Culture A.D. 500-1500, ed. R. R. Bolgar (Cambridge, 1971) 83-94. William of Conches' glosses on Juvenal were edited by B. Wilson, Guillaume De Conches Glosae in Juvenalem (Paris, 1980).

[11] An important study of parody, with numerous examples, is P. Lehmann, Die Parodie im Mittelalter (Stuttgart, 1963 repr.).

[12] D. S. Wiesen, St. Jerome as a Satirist (Ithaca, 1964).

[13] The quotation is from Ronald A. Knox, "On Humour and Satire," in Satire: Modern Essays in Criticism, ed. R. Paulson (Englewood Cliffs, N.J., 1971).

[14] J. A. Yunck, The Lineage of Lady Meed: The Development of Mediaeval Venality Satire (South Bend, Indiana, 1963).

[15] The text is I.1, number 44, in A. Hilka, O. Schumann and B. Bischoff, eds. Carmina Burana 2 vols. (Heidelberg, 1930-70). See also Jill Mann, "Satiric Subject and Satiric Object in Goliardic Literature, " Mittellateinisches Jahrbuch 15 (1980) 63-86, esp. 74-77.

[16] Wilchard's poem was printed by Mathias Flacius Illyricus in Varia doctorum piorumque virorum de corrupto Ecclesiae Statu Poemata (Basel, 1557), but it has been mistakenly attributed to other authors, e.g., T. Wright, Anglo-Latin Satirists and Epigrammatists of the Twelfth Century, (London, 1872) assigns it to Gualo the Briton, while in PL 171 it is printed among the carmina varia of Marbod of Rennes. "De vita monachorum" is ascribed to Roger of Caen by J. H. Mozley, "The Unprinted Poems of Nigel Wireker," Speculum 7 (1932) 398-423.

[17] J. H. Mozley and R. R. Raymo, Nigel de Longchamps Speculum Stultorum (Berkeley, CA, 1960) 6.

[18] For example, see 7.23 of Joannis Saresberiensis Episcopi Carnotensis Policratici, ed. C. C. J. Webb, 2 vols, (Oxford, 1909), and Gerald of Wales' Speculum Ecclesiae (Bk. 3) in Giraldi

Cambrensis Opera, eds. J. S. Brewer, J. Dimock and G. F. Warner (London, 1861-91).

[19]M. R. James, rev. by C.N.L. Brooke and R. A. B. Mynors, Walter Map De Nugis Curialium (Oxford, 1983) 84. See also the articles by Lewis Thorpe, "Walter Map and Gerald of Wales," Medium Aevum XLVII (1978, no. 1) 6-21, and Michael Richter, "Gerald of Wales," Traditio XXIX (1973) 379-90.

[20]L. J. Paetow, ed. Two Medieval Satires on the University of Paris: La Bataille des VII Arts of Henri D'Andeli and the Morale Scolarium of John of Garland (Berkeley, CA., 1927).

[21]R. R. Bolgar, The Classical Heritage (N.Y., 1964 repr.) 215-22. See also Hans Liebeschütz, Medieval Humanism in the Life and Writings of John of Salisbury (London, 1950) 90-94.

[22]C. C. J. Webb, ed. Joannis Saresberiensis Episcopi Carnotensis Metalogicon (Oxford, 1929). See D. D. McGarry, "Educational Theory in the Metalogicon of John of Salisbury," Speculum 23 (1948) 659-75, and J. O. Ward, "The Date of the Commentary on Cicero's 'De Inventione' by Thierry of Chartres (ca. 1095-1160?) and the Cornifician Attack on the Liberal Arts," Viator 3 (1972) 219-73. A less reliable article on the subject is Rosemary Barton Tobin, "The Cornifician Motif in John of Salisbury's Metalogicon," History of Education 13 (1984) 1-6. Ms. Tobin mistakenly claims that the Metalogicon is addressed to "Cornificius."

[23]Ronald E. Pepin, "The 'Entheticus' of John of Salisbury: A Critical Text," Traditio XXXI (1975) 139. John's poem, which amply displays his abiding fondness for pseudonyms, was composed over a period of time, some surely during his own school days or shortly after.

[24]The same theme is addressed in the Policraticus, which John subtitled "De nugis curialium et vestigiis philosophorum."

[25]A. Boutemy, ed. Nigellus de Longchamp dit Wireker Tractatus Contra Curiales et Officiales Clericos (Paris, 1959).

[26]The quotation is from Paetow, 53. John dedicated his poem to Walter de Coutances, newly elected (1184) Archbishop of Rouen. The critical edition is P. G. Schmidt, Johannes de Hauvilla Architrenius (Munich, 1974). W. Wetherbee briefly discusses the

poem's content and meaning in Platonism and Poetry in the Twelfth Century (Princeton, 1972) 242-55.

[27] De nugis curialium 5.7: curia locus est penalis; infernum mea non dico, sed fere tantam habet ad ipsum similitudinem quantam equi ferrum ad eque.

[28] For example, Francis Utley, The Crooked Rib (Columbus, Ohio, 1944); H. R. Mays, The Dangerous Sex (N.Y., 1964); Katharine Rogers, The Troublesome Helpmate (University of Washington, 1966); Vern L. Bullough, The Subordinate Sex (Urbana, Illinois, 1973).

[29] L. Van Acker, ed. Petri Pictoris Carmina in Corpus Christianorum (Continuatio Mediaevalis) XXV (Turnholt, 1972) 166.

[30] Marbod's "De meretrice" is in PL 171, 1698-99; some misogynistic pieces attributed to Hildebert are in the same volume, 1428-30. "De tribus vitiis" is in Hildeberti Cenomanensis Episcopi Carmina Minora, ed. A. Brian Scott (Leipzig, 1969) 40-42.

[31] G. R. Owst, Literature and Pulpit in Medieval England (Cambridge, 1933) 375-404.

[32] "The Nightingale and the Thrush" is printed (#59) among the Middle English Lyrics, eds. M. S. Luria and R. L. Hoffman (N.Y., 1974) 56-61. See lines 2414ff. in Sir Gawain and the Green Knight, eds. J. R. R. Tolkien and E. V. Gordon, rev. by N. Davis (Oxford, 1967).

[33] H. C. Thomas, ed. Philobiblon Ricardi de Bury (Oxford, 1970) 44; F. N. Robinson, ed. The Works of Geoffrey Chaucer (Boston, 1957) 82.

[34] Mozley and Raymo, 6.

[35] Wright, vol. 2, 164-66.

[36] This poem was edited by R. B. C. Huygens in Studi Medievali 3rd series, #3 (1962) 765-72.

[37] H. Watenphul and H. Krefeld, Die Gedichte des Archipoeta (Heidelberg, 1958) 73-77. The poem is discussed by Jill Mann in the article cited above, and by Francis Cairns, "The Archpoet's

Confession: Sources, Interpretation and Historical Context," Mittellateinisches Jahrbuch 15 (1980) 87-103.

[38]W. J. Millor and H. E. Butler, rev. by C.N.L. Brooke, The Letters of John of Salisbury Vol. 1 (London, 1955). The humorous aspects of John's correspondence with Peter of Celle are treated by R. E. Pepin, "Amicitia Jocosa: Peter of Celle and John of Salisbury," Florilegium 5 (1983) 140-56. The epistles of Peter of Blois are in PL 207. Two studies of his letters are R. W. Southern, "Peter of Blois: a Twelfth-Century Humanist?" in Medieval Humanism and Other Studies (N.Y., 1970) 105-32, and Ethel C. Higonnet, "Spiritual Ideas in the Letters of Peter of Blois," Speculum L (April, 1975) 218-44.

[39]Peter's list resembles that of John of Salisbury's Policraticus 8.13.

[40]The work is printed in PL 182, 895-918. See Jean Leclercq, "Aspects littéraires de l'oeuvre de S. Bernard, Un modèle du genre satirique," Cahiers de la civilization médiévale (1958) 444-50.

[41]Janet Martin, ed. Peter the Venerable: Selected Letters (Toronto, 1974) 85.

CHAPTER II

BERNARD OF MORVAL

> **Hora novissima, tempora pessima sunt, vigilemus**
>
> - Bernard of Morval -

By reputation, Bernard of Morval is the very caricature of the medieval monk aspiring to eternal rewards and despising the fleeting pleasures of this life. His vision of celestial bliss and his loathing of the world find expression in a poem of almost three thousand hexameter lines, divided into three cantos of almost equal length, entitled <u>De contemptu mundi</u>.[1] Written before the middle of the twelfth century and dedicated to his abbot, Peter the Venerable, Bernard's work came to enjoy considerable popularity, as evidenced by a good number of manuscript copies in the thirteenth and fourteenth centuries. The first printed edition in 1557, and several thereafter, had wide appeal to Protestants who found the author's fulminations against ecclesiastical abuses, especially the third canto's attacks on Rome, most congenial to their cause of reformation. Thus, he became to them a patron saint who, according to his second editor, Nathan Chytraeus (Bremen, 1597), castigated most severely the abominations and crimes of the clergy, the curia and the pope. The third editor, Eilhard Lubin (Rostock, 1610), voiced similar sentiments in his preface, and went on to wonder what this good monk would have said about "the last plague let loose upon a crumbling world, these locusts, these cancers of the human race - the Jesuits."[2]

A second area of widespread influence for Bernard's poem, or, more accurately, the opening lines of the first book, is hymnody. His vision of the heavenly city has often found a place in collections of sacred songs, particularly in the nineteenth century. The most famous rendering of Bernard's verses, more an imitation than a translation, is The Rhythm of Bernard de Morlaix, monk of Cluny, on the Celestial Country, by J. M. Neale. The Rev. Neale's little book saw eight editions between 1859 and 1866. The poem even inspired an original musical score for soli, chorus and orchestra entitled Hora Novissima, composed by Horatio W. Parker for the Church Choral Society of New York in 1893.[3]

Little can be claimed with certainty about our Bernard, besides the fact that he was a monk of Cluny. In keeping with monastic tradition, he intruded no personal details in his poetry. His dates, birthplace and activities beyond the poem are unknown, though we can safely place his work in the second quarter of the twelfth century, thanks to its prefatory letter to Abbot Peter (d. 1156). Several other compositions, including "Mariale," a famous hymn to the Virgin, have been ascribed to Bernard, but without compelling evidence.[4] Of course, the commonality of the name Bernard in the Middle Ages has contributed to the confusion about our author, who has at times been mistakenly identified with Bernard of Clairvaux. Though his most recent editor has made a strong case, based on manuscript evidence, for calling him Bernard of Morval, he has in the past been cited most often as Bernard of Morlas or Bernard of Cluny.

In most surviving manuscripts of De contemptu mundi, there appears the dedicatory epistle to Peter the Venerable. It offers some conventional observations on the prudence of submitting one's work to careful correction and enlightened criticism. Bernard cites classical authorities, chiefly Horace's Ars Poetica, for these views. He also expresses quite plainly his reasons for composing the poem, acknowledges his reputation for verse among contemporaries, and declares that scarcely anyone reproaches vices in speech or in writing. Thus, he states, the heart within him is burning to do so.[5] He affirms that the Lord has filled him with a spirit of wisdom and understanding, for without this inspiration he would have never sustained such a lengthy work in so difficult a metre. Before closing, Bernard records his subject (materia) and purpose (intentio). They are traditional in satire: reproach of vices and recall from vices (viciorum reprehensio et a viciis revocare).

His poem of 2,966 lines remains the most elaborate medieval composition on a popular theme. Many authors, before and after Bernard, have discoursed upon the miseries of human life and expressed, often eloquently, their sorrow for the human condition. For the Christian preacher or writer, contemptus mundi involves reflection upon two consequences of Man's fall: the suffering he endures as a result of the first sin (mala poenae), and the evils he perpetuates as a guilty child of Adam and Eve (mala culpae).[6] Most surviving works in this genre are litanies of woe designed to annihilate pride and inspire meditation on death and eternity. Some of them detail human iniquity and call to repentance. Many conclude with descriptions of the final judgment and visions of everlasting punishment or reward. Twelfth-century examples include the prose De miseria conditionis humanae of Lotario Dei Segni (later Pope Innocent III), and the briefer Dialogus de mundi contemptu vel amore attributed to Conrad of Hirsau.[7] Poems in the genre have been ascribed to Anselm of Canterbury and Bernard of Clairvaux. Recently, the poem "Mundus deciduus" was edited and attributed to Alan of Lille.[8] The theme was pervasive in the writings of the historian, Henry of Huntingdon, who also wrote ninety elegiac verses on contempt of the world.[9] No work of the twelfth century, however, can compare favorably in detailed content and poetic force to the De contemptu mundi of Bernard of Morval.

The Scriptural authority for contemptus mundi resides in the first epistle of Saint John (2:15-18). There the author cautions his disciples against love of the world and the things of the world, for they are filled with concupiscence and pride. He announces that the final hour, hora novissima, is at hand, and he predicts the imminent appearance of Antichrist. Bernard of Morval distinctly echoes this passage in the opening line of the poem:

> Hora novissima, tempora pessima sunt, vigilemus.
> The final hour, the worst times are here -- be watchful.

These words, which both open and close the first canto, establish the three themes which the poet will elaborate: the last judgment, Man's iniquity, and repentance. The second of these lends itself traditionally to satire. I shall consider the persona of De contemptu mundi and the abuses he scores after a brief overview of the poem as a whole.

The first canto, the longest, proceeds rapidly from the opening announcement of the great conflagration and final judgment to a promise of heavenly joys (gaudia coelica). For almost four hundred lines, the poet describes the rewards awaiting the faithful in Urbs Sion, the celestial city so perfectly emblematic of the monastic vocation.[10] There Jesus, the just judge, will bestow the fullness of peace (plena refectio), light and love upon the blessed. After a transitional summons to repentance, Bernard commences an equally long rehearsal of eternal punishments for the damned. His depictions of the suffering in Hell are impersonal and lack the detail of Dante's Inferno, but they are amply vivid and gloomy. Though Bernard explicitly rejects the classical underworld of Vergil's Aeneid ("Non ibi navita, cymbaque praedita voce Maronis"), he does unfold before his reader a horrifying place of fire, ice, stench, demons, gorgons, worms and flaming dragons, hammers and fiery torrents, shadows, gnashing teeth, whips, burning chains, and more. Bernard concludes his awful vision with the observation that the mighty of this world are cast down into torment, and this leads him to another convention of contemptus mundi, the ubi sunt? theme. He devotes nearly three hundred lines to the vanities of the world, the brevity of life, and, in particular, to the lost grandeur of Rome. Finally, the poet completes his circle by returning to manifest signs of the final judgment. The evils and aberrations of the day herald the arrival of Antichrist and the end of the world. Vigilemus.

The second and third cantos interest us more, from a satirical point of view. In these, the poet assails contemporary abuses. His theme is introduced by the words,

> The age of gold and our first strength have passed away
> (Aurea tempora, primaque robora, praeterierunt)

In terms reminiscent of the classical poets, especially Ovid, Bernard describes the Golden Age, the hardy race nourished by acorns, the land of milk and honey, the days of harmony and peace. This serene era is depicted, of course, to contrast his own degenerate times. In an extended first person address, the poet declares (twice) that he must compose satire:

> Evils stand, Right retires, hence a wide way opens to satire;
> Grant pardon, I pray, here I follow satire . . .
>
> (Stant mala, jus latet, hinc satirae patet area lata;
> Da veniam precor; hic satiram sequor . . .)
> (II. 130 and 133)

The remainder of the second canto is a relentless mockery of a wicked age, including an ironic depiction of the estates from kings to farmers, a vehement attack on "wicked women," hypocrisy, avarice and other rampant vices. It concludes with the poet's weary admission that in describing further the world's wickedness, his paper, his words, his time would run out. With Ovid (<u>Ars Amatoria</u> I.722), he declares:

We race over deep seas, now let the anchor be cast
(Alta per aequora currimus anchora nunc jaciatur)
(II. 973)

The poet weighs anchor in the third canto, and continues to deride the folly and depravity of <u>mala tempora</u>. Among his major objects of harsh ridicule are fraud, sodomy, episcopal luxury, simony and venality at Rome, where <u>Pecunia</u> reigns. The poet concludes his lengthy work with the commonplace acknowledgement of his inability to do justice to his theme:

To reproach you and declare your infamies I have wished.
To reproach you and declare your infamies I was unable.

(Vos ego carpere, vestraque dicere probra cupivi,
Vos ego carpere, vestraque dicere probra nequivi)
(III. 887-88)

Thus, he invites his readers to moral reform, to the narrow way, and ends with a prayer for the restoration of the Golden Age:

Restore the Golden Age and our first strengh we beg,
Now guide us, hereafter gather us, lest we perish.

(Aurea tempora, primaque robora redde, rogamus.
Nos modo dirige, postmodo collige, ne pereamus)
(III. 913-14)

Just as the first canto had opened and closed with <u>hora novissima</u>, the last two cantos, taken together, form a unit beginning and ending with <u>aurea tempora</u>. The degeneracy of the world prompts the poet to adopt the satirical mode in these cantos, as he explicitly states, in a way that is not present in the first. The initial book of <u>De contemptu mundi</u> might lead its reader to agree with Charles Witke that the work "approaches more closely to rhetorical invective expanded to boring length than to satire."[11] However, the remainder of the poem conforms much more to traditional satire, and in it Bernard creates a distinctive satirical <u>persona</u>.

Throughout his lengthy work the poet interjects first person comments, the conventional <u>Icherzahlung</u> of satire. In fact, he does so more than eighty times in the entire poem, with over sixty instances, notably, in the last two cantos, the satirical books. Of course many interjections are merely rhetorical questions, such as "quid moror?" or standard affirmations of the poet's own small ability, as in "ego paupere pauper avena." Such formulas are not restricted to satire, but there are much more telling outbursts by the poet of <u>De contemptu mundi</u> which may offer starting points for a discussion of the satiric <u>persona</u>.

First, there is indignation, and it occurs in full Juvenalian measure. At several places in his description of folly and iniquity, Bernard declares that he trembles at such sights. "Dum loquor, horreo" is a frequent exclamation. Just as often, our poet invokes the imagery of flame to express his seething disgust for unchecked vices, and the reader becomes accustomed to "cremor," "uror," and "excoquor." No wonder Bernard's editor was prompted to describe him as "red hot against the evils of his time."[12] In a few places, the poet combined these images to produce a line such as,

> I shudder to tell what I am often burning to reproach
> (Horreo dicere quae reprehendere saepe reflammor)
>
> (III. 429)

Righteous indignation, the legacy of early Juvenalian satire, is acknowledged by the speaker as the proper temperament for the satirical voice of De contemptu mundi. At one point, Bernard places himself in this tradition of classical satire when he asks,

> Horace and Cato, Persius and Juvenal, I ask,
> What would they do now, if the common life were theirs?
> Lucilius himself would be stunned at today's deeds,
> And would proclaim his own age fortunate and blessed.
>
> (Flaccus Horatius et Cato Persius et Juvenalis
> Quid facerent rogo, si foret his modo vita sodalis?
> Temporis istius acta Lucilius ille stuperet,
> Et sua prospera sanctaque tempora non reticeret)
>
> (II. 805-80)

Bernard's kinship to Roman satire, especially Juvenal, is further evidenced by his frequent borrowing of phrases, names, themes, and images. When he exclaims, "ardeo carpere," he reminds us of Juvenal, for whom ardere (to burn) was a favorite word (used 26 times in his brief collection of poems). Other familiar Juvenalian expressions, such as Venus ignea, vacuus canit, and sportula plena are employed many times in his work, almost all in the second and third cantos. Admittedly, many classical lines had become proverbial by Bernard's time, but his special fondness for

Juvenal, and Horace, is evident in numerous allusions which reveal a familiarity with the entire corpus of their satires.

Our poet often declares his satiric intention, by explicitly affirming it, as we have noted, and by the vocabulary he employs to describe his work. A fourth-century grammarian, Diomedes, actually following Suetonius, had defined satire as carmen maledicum et ad carpenda hominum vitia compositum.[13] Along with verbs meaning to bite or gnaw, such as rodere and mordere, carpere is discovered often among satirists who describe their own efforts to reproach vices. In the twelfth century, for example, Walter of Chatillon repeatedly underscores his satirical thrusts with these words. I think it helps us to understand better our poet and his intention when we recognize that he too employs this satiric vocabulary widely in first person passages. With some frequency the reader encounters expressions such as ardeo carpere; carmine mordeo; crimina rodere; talia mordeo. All such expressions in De contemptu mundi are confined to the second and third cantos.

If the persona of Bernard's poem identifies himself with the satiric genre and its great Roman masters, he also evidences that charity which must, of necessity, impose limitations on the Christian writer. He may hate the sin, but he must love the sinner. He may rail against vices, but he must mourn their everlasting consequences for his brethren. His indignation and ridicule must be tempered by tears of profound remorse. Our poet attempted to articulate this dilemma in the verse:

> I lament, I laugh, I am Diogenes, I am Democritus.
> (Lugeo, rideo, Diogenes ego, Democritus sum)
>
> (II. 392)

For Bernard, virulent invective must be linked to moral reform, the one symbolized by lacerating teeth and the other by streaming tears. This outlook accounts for the abundant tears in <u>De contemptu mundi</u>. For as frequently as the reader encounters the affirmations of satiric reproach in the second and third cantos, he also meets with a melancholy born of charity and expressed plainly in verbs of weeping. Often <u>fleo</u> or <u>lugeo</u> will announce, or conclude, a passage in which the poet censors a particular iniquity, as in this lugubrious example:

> While I speak, I weep, weeping I grieve, I lament, I sigh,
> I weep over these defiled by love of power, those by lust.
>
> (Dum loquor haec, fleo, flendo dolens eo, plango, gemisco,
> Haec fleo culminis illa libidinis oblita visco)
>
> (III. 163-64)

These tears, of course, do much to legitimize Christian satire. They help to elevate the <u>persona</u> of <u>De contemptu mundi</u> to that superior moral position from which every satirist must look down upon the world beneath, but they further serve to endow his work with brotherly love. In this aspect of satire, Bernard is less akin to Juvenal, more to Jerome, whose instrument for reform was bitter satire.[14]

If Bernard established for his poem a <u>persona</u> who balances satiric zeal with Christian charity, he also provided him with splendid erudition in secular and sacred lore. The satirist must always be morally superior to those whom he reproaches, even if he is poorer, or younger, or outcast. Usually he is wiser, more insightful and wittier than those he scorns. Often his lofty posture depends, in part, on a display of wide learning and rich experience. The speaker in <u>De contemptu mundi</u> is impressively well educated. Of course, he demonstrates a thorough familiarity with the sacred page. The poem is replete with allusions to Scripture. Verbal echoes of <u>Psalms</u>, <u>Job</u>, the prophets, the evangelists, epistles and <u>Apocalypse</u> abound in the work. Many expressions can be traced to the Fathers as well, though none are ever named. Only Pope Gregory I, whom the poet calls "Gregorius meus," receives a brief encomium. Its brevity, however, is amply compensated by effusion. Bernard affirms that God speaks through the mouth of Gregory, whose glory will remain forever, and he concludes:

> Now will his golden, fiery pen by no means die;
> By his offshoots will be taken up the golden page.
> When Platos and Ciceros are taken to Stygian realms,
> He, snatched to Heaven, will live in God's bosom.
> He should be reread, carefully and faithfully,
> But the pen of pagan and poet must be cast away.
>
> (Jam stylus aureus ejus et igneus haud morietur,
> Aurea pagina per sua germina suscipietur.
> Ille Platonibus et Ciceronibus ad Stygia raptis,
> Raptus ad aethera, vivit ad ubera stans Deitatis,

> Hic specialiter atque fideliter est relegendus,
> Sed stylus ethnicus atque poeticus abjiciendus)
>
> (III. 313-18)

The closing sentiment quoted above, namely that pagan literature must be rejected by the Christian writer, signals the age-old dilemma of Jerome the Ciceronian, of Augustine weeping over Dido. These <u>auctores</u> had reconciled themselves to their literary educations with allegories of the <u>captiva gentilis</u> of <u>Deuteronomy</u> (21:10-13) and <u>Spoliatio Aegyptiorum</u> of <u>Exodus</u> (12:35-36), but many monastic writers after them felt obliged to disparage secular learning, especially poetic fables. By the twelfth century, such declarations had become <u>pro forma</u>. Thus, Bernard includes in his satiric discourse occasional barbs at the classics which so richly inform his own content and expression. Vergil is wrong ("O Maro, falleris") and Socrates too verbose ("Socrates garrula"). Pagan works have supplanted divine learning in school:

> Who now toils that divine letters be taught as pagan are?
> (Quis modo coelica sudat ut ethnica scripta doceri?)
>
> (III. 259)

These conventional reproaches are aimed, I am confident, at Bernard's cloistered brothers who pursue the arts too avidly for advancement, while neglecting their divine offices. In fact, one telling couplet confirms this:

> Who argues well and reckons swiftly by scholar's craft,
> Seeks not to become Abbot by deeds, but by the arts.

> (Qui bene disputat et cito computat arte scholari
> Non petit actibus at petit artibus abba creari)
>
> (III. 297-98)

These infrequent cliches, however, cannot dispel the aura of classical erudition in the verses of De contemptu mundi. The poet repeatedly punctuates his satire with references to an impressive array of ancient materials. Many of the tags he borrowed from Roman poets were common enough in school exercises of the day, to be sure, but their range and extent are extraordinary for a monastic author. In addition to the satirists and Vergil, who are named, our poet draws liberally upon Terence, the Disticha Catonis, Cicero, Sallust, Pliny, and Lucan, among others. He borrows frequently from Ovid, especially Metamorphoses, Heroides and Ars Amatoria. His use of names and places, both actual and mythical, is too widespread to detail here, but one finds them on every page of the text. The gods and heroes, rivers and winds, people and sites of antiquity are discovered throughout the poem of this monk who disparaged the fabulae poeticae.

Although the scope of this introduction to the satirical aspects of De contemptu mundi precludes a deeper analysis of the poet's classical education, we can pause to note his predilection for combining scriptural and classical examples. Of course, the supreme medieval fusion of these traditions awaited Dante a century and a half later, and Bernard's occasional blending of them cannot approach the extraordinary synthesis of La Commedia. However, Bernard does bear witness to the celebrated classical revival of the twelfth century. His tendency to illustrate a point with combined examples enables him to display wider erudition and, more importantly, to reinforce his argument from a double authority. Thus, for example, his attack on homosexuality (III. 177-220) includes as many references to Ganymede as to Sodom and Gomorrha. Hell has the fire of gehenna and the Stygian waves; the wiles of women ruined Joseph and Hippolytus; the strength of young manhood was lost to Absalom and Hector. When our satirist declaims against sexual degeneracy, he employs a symbol from each tradition in a single line:

> Juno is abandoned, and Petronilla herself is rejected.
> (Juno relinquitur, ipsa repellitur et Petronilla)
>
> (III. 182)

The former, of course, was the Roman patroness of marriage, and the latter a saintly exemplar of virginity. Though such combinations are brief, and rarely elaborated in the poem, they occur frequently enough to demonstrate clearly the Christian, indeed, the monastic accomodation of classical letters. The practice enhances the stature of the persona, challenges his readers, and lends force to his critical outpourings.

Bernard's satirical sweep missed nothing of the degeneracy of his days. Satire, by nature, exaggerates, and our poet liberally indulges this requirement. The expressions O mala tempora and mala secula are used so often that readers of De contemptu mundi might well imagine our poet on a street corner carrying a huge sign proclaiming the end of the world and railing at every passerby. The tendency of modern critics has been to view the poem as a Jeremiad, a deadly-earnest attempt to preach reform. Its editors have always taken it that way. The few published studies of the piece have lingered over its eschatological thrust, and the scriptural foundations of its wider theme, contempt for the world.[15] All note the satiric genre, but none really view the poem as such, nor do they distinguish between the cantos, which I think is essential. They have allowed for hyperbole, but not humor. None have noted that each time the outcry O mala tempora! is raised, a new satirical subject is being announced. The phrase is more than an anguished outburst; it is also a transitional device. With satirical exaggeration in mind, then, I shall survey briefly some major objects of Bernard's scathing attacks.

First, we should recall that the second canto opens and the third canto closes with a reminiscence of the Golden Age. Horace had used the theme more than once, and Juvenal liked to contrast the peace and bounty of old with the violence and corruption of imperial Rome. So, also, Bernard employs the legendary past to set in sharper relief the decadence of his own times. Curiously, he does not identify the Golden Age with Eden before the Fall, but his imagery is classical, mostly Ovidian. Within this framework of the Golden Age, the poet assails every imaginable vice, after pausing at the outset (ll. 123-62) to reveal his mood (seething with anger and weeping with regret) and his method (he must write satire). The suggestion once made that Bernard invoked the aurea tempora "merely as a premise for satire on women" is a misleading oversimplification which suggests that its author did not read the entire poem.[16]

After the introduction to the second canto, Bernard proceeds to a satira communis, or general satire on the classes of society. The form was popular among Anglo-Latin writers of the century, notably Nigel of Canterbury and Henry of Huntingdon.[17] The estates are paraded forth, beginning with bishops and descending to farmers. In all, nine professions are summoned for review: <u>Praesul</u> (bishop); <u>Sceptriger</u> (king); <u>Presbyter</u> (priest); <u>Clericus</u> (cleric); <u>Miles</u> (soldier); <u>Nobilis</u> (nobleman); <u>Censor</u> (judge); <u>Institor</u> (agent, or merchant); <u>Rusticus</u> (farmer). Our poet goes on to deride the failings of each in turn, after announcing his satiric intention:

> In repeating separate sins more widely and extensively,
> I increase reflection, and I strive to disparage them.
>
> (Singula latius et spaciocius haec repetendo,
> Addo revolvere criminaque rodere denuo tendo.)
> (ll. 259-60)

For example, the bishop, caring naught for souls, loves glory, pomp and riches. The king is cruel, the priest lax and lecherous, the cleric, a far cry from Chaucer's studious young man, neglects his sacred calling to become an ambitious courtier. The follies of each estate are sharply and cleverly detailed. Observe, for instance, how alliteration underscores the haste, the frenzy of the merchant's life:

> Through dark cold, over mountains, through markets, over seas he rushes,
> A thief seizes, an enemy strikes him, winter wears him down, summer burns him up.
> Captured, poor, he goes off and emptyhanded sings before the robber;
> He renews his gains, and hence hastens his journey into Babylon.

> (Per nigra frigora, per juga, per fora per freta currit;
> Fur capit, hunc ferit hostis hiems terit, aestus adurit.
> Captus, egens abit, et vacuus canit ante latronem,
> Lucra resuscitat, hinc iter incitat in Babylonem)
>
> (II. 347-50)

The poet demonstrates through the <u>satira communis</u> that none live up to their calling. The world is populated, in his words, by a <u>gens asinaria</u> unable to curb its desires, a <u>gens ebria</u> which cannot distinguish the purchase of a meal from the buying of a whore's favors (II. 397-98).

The next major theme for our poet is wicked women. He employs the satiric vocabulary once again for a brief <u>apologia</u> at the outset of this passage:

> I am not going to revile upright women whom I ought bless,
> but since I must, in my poem I sting those of Locusta's mind.
> Now wicked woman becomes my theme, becomes my satire.
> Herself I approve, but her deeds reproach and thus pursue.
>
> (Non eo carpere quas benedicere debeo justas
> Sed quia debeo carmine mordeo mente Locustas.
> Nunc mala foemina fit mihi pagina fit mihi sermo.
> Se satis approbo, sed sua reprobo, persequar ergo)
>
> (II. 449-52)

Then, echoing much in Juvenal, Bernard indulges in unrelieved misogyny for one hundred and fifty lines. His exaggerations are ludicrous, his epithets vehement and obscene. The wicked woman is likened to the lioness, the she-wolf, the night-owl, the serpent and the dragon. She offers brief delight, long suffering. She adorns herself for deception, this destroyer of John the Baptist, Samson, Joseph, Adam, Hippolytus, and a host more. She would rather have one eye than one man! Bernard even follows Juvenal (VI. 592ff.) in denouncing abortion as well as adultery. In all of this, our poet accedes to a commonplace of clerical writers which long antedated the twelfth century and long survived it. Almost identical formulas and epithets are discovered in other poets of the period, as we have seen of Marbod of Rennes, Hildebert of Lavardin, and Petrus Pictor.[18] Here is a sample of Bernard's contribution to this popular satirical theme:

> Woman induces wickedness by nods, skills, deeds;
> She is glad to compel sins, to live wholly woman.
> Indeed, no woman is good, yet if any happens to be so,
> The good is bad, for almost no woman is good.
> Woman is a guilty thing, wickedly carnal, all flesh,
> Quick to betray, born to deceive, taught to deceive.
> The lowest ditch, the worst serpent, lovely rottenness,
> A slippery path, a wickedly common thing, a plunderer,
> A bristly night-owl, a common doorway, sweet poison,
> Knowing nothing well, fickle, wicked, a vessel of decay,
> A vessel less useful, more violable, shameful,
> Insatiable, irreconcilable, quarrelsome.
> Merchandise sold for a trifle, quickly lost, slave of gold,
> A passionate flame, she loves to deceive and be deceived.

She is an enemy to lovers, a friend to enemies.
Unless sought, she seeks, and reaps profits unjustly.
At night are her joys, her own, her day is night.
She excludes nothing; she conceives of a father, a nephew.
A pit of lust, arms of the abyss, a mouth of vices
She was, is, will be; through her good order perishes.
As long as crops granted to farmers grow in the country,
This lioness will roar, this beast will rage against justice.
She is final madness, the enemy within, the nearest plague.
While she refuses, she entices, brings sin to the virtuous.
She is all flesh, but in decay; by her inconstancy, Proteus
She surpasses, and in her impiety, she is thought pious.
She teaches vice; my verse will not call her vicious;
I call her a vice, I prove her a treachery, a crime.
She is a great commodity, the worst of all possible things.
The art of women becomes more wary than all other arts.
A she-wolf is no more harmful, since her attack is sparing,
Nor a dragon, nor lion -- but what can I call worse than she?
All her acts, not only guilty, but good, you may condemn.
John the Baptist accused her crime and died by the sword.
Because of her Hippolytus also fell, Ammon fell,
Because of her Joseph is confined and your locks shorn, Samson,
Because of her Ruben, David, Solomon, Adam sink down.
She gives, acts, bears herself so that decency perishes -- whence we perish.

(Foemina nutibus artibus actibus impia suadet,
Cogere crimina, totaque foemina vivere gaudet.
Nulla quidem bona, si tamen et bona contigit ulla,

Est mala res bona, namque fere bona foemina nulla.
Foemina res rea, res male carnea, vel caro tota,
Strenua prodere, nataque fallere, fallere docta.
Fossa novissima, vipera pessima, pulchra putredo,
Semita lubrica, res male publica, praedaque praedo,
Horrida noctua, publica janua, dulce venenum.
Nil bene conscia, mobilis, impia, vas lue plenum,
Vas minus utile, plus violabile, flagitiosum,
Insatiabile, dissociabile, litigiosum.
Merx leve vendita, sed cito perdita, serva metalli,
Flamma domestica, diligit unica fallere falli.
Extat amantibus hostis, et hostibus extat amica.
Ni petitur petit, idque lucre metit ut sit iniqua.
Sunt sua gaudia, sunt sua propria, lux sua nocte.
Haec nihil excipit, ex patre concipit, exque nepote;
Fossa libidinis, arma voraginis, os vitiorum
Haec fuit, est, erit, et per eam perit ordo bonorum.
Donec erunt sata ruricolis data, credita ruri,
Haec lea rugiet, haec fera saeviet obvia juri.
Haec furor ultimus, hostis et intimus, intima pestis.
Dum negat illicit, et scelus injicit ipsa modestis.
Haec caro carnea, sed lue Protea mobilitate
Vincere noscitur, haec pia cernitur impietate.
Haec vitium docet, ars mea non vocet hanc vitiosam;
Hanc vitium voco, perfidiam probo, nomino noxam.
Merx ea plurima, res ea pessima, pessima rerum,
Cautior omnibus una fit artibus ars mulierum.
Non lupa nequior hac, quia parcior impetus ejus.
Non draco, non leo, sed quid ea queo dicere peius?
Istius omnia non modo noxia sed bona dampnes.

> Hoc scelus arguit, enseque corruit ille Johannes.
> Hac quoque vir fuit Hippolytus ruit, hac ruit Ammon,
> Hac Joseph angitur, et coma raditur hac tua, Samson.
> Hac Ruben, hac David, hac Salomon cadit, hac homo primus.
> Haec dat, agit, gerit, unde pudor perit -- unde perimus.)
>
> (II. 453-90)

Why did Bernard of Morval conform to the excesses of this convention? Jerome and other Christian apologists did so, we are assured, to promote asceticism and the ideal of dedicated virginity.[19] Such might have been our poet's motive as well, but I suspect that it was not. To be sure, his satire was intended to censor human folly in all its manifestations, but also to ridicule, to make people laugh, even if uneasily. At many points in his long work, the poet addresses his reader (and listener), as we have noted. As the long section on wicked women draws to its conclusion, he pauses to say:

> Such things I sting, at such I laugh, but with weeping.
> (Talia mordeo, talia rideo, non sine fletu)
>
> (II. 540)

The line clearly reinforces satire in the verb <u>mordere</u>, humor in <u>ridere</u>, and Christian zeal for reform in <u>fletu</u>. One imagines that his audience shared the laughter. S. M. Jackson, writing about this passage, speculated, "how the monks must have roared as they heard those lines read! How often the author must have stopped in his reading to remark that he did not speak altogether seriously!"[20] I am convinced that Bernard's exaggerated antifeminism is not a polemic on behalf of monastic chastity, nor the rantings of a fanatic, but rather it represents his contribution to a stereotyped genre, another legacy of Juvenal and Jerome. Though his poetry is masterful and inventive, its misogynistic content is cliched, and Bernard surely realized that. He composed a stinging lampoon on a well-worked satirical theme, which is precisely why the author himself would say of it, "talia rideo."

In the remainder of the second canto (563-974), Bernard does not focus at length on particular objects of satire, but rather ranges widely over societal maladies. The deadly sins and all their progeny run rampant in his panorama of decadence. <u>Superbia</u> beseiges human hearts, and her howling troop takes up her commands. <u>Venus ebria</u> (another Juvenalian image) holds sway to such an extent that mere boys become fathers, little girls long for babies, and, in consequence, the world is overpopulated. There is no peace, even among Christians, in a world where hypocrisy and avarice reign.

The poet's rapid, discursive treatment of themes in the second canto offers the reader a <u>satura lanx</u>, a full platter of satirical dishes. He has assembled the wide array of faults and failings to expose them, to mock them, and to correct them. That they were exaggerated, perhaps beyond credibility, Bernard knew, and sometimes said so:

> Here I am more foolishly pretending -- but they are like that!
> (Insipientior, hic ego mentior, at simulantur)
> (II. 734)

The third canto of De contemptu mundi is a piece with the second. In it the poet continues the reproach and the ridicule which characterized the previous book. At times, his assault on vice is general, as when he exposes the reign of Fraud everywhere, or quite pointed, as in his severe attack on homosexuality (177-220). Perhaps the only noticeable difference between the two cantos is that the final one addresses mainly ecclesiastical abuses, while the former surveyed chiefly secular themes. Thus, as one might expect, there is a diatribe on simony (506-94), another on the preferment of beardless boys in the ranks of the Church (391-414), and, longest of all, a fierce denunciation of corruption at Rome (595-746). The latter was, of course, another convention of medieval writers, as John Yunck has demonstrated in his book on venality satire. Yunck is right in pronouncing that Bernard "says nothing that we have not heard before," though his remark takes no account of the poet's brilliance of expression.[21]

Surely the finest and funniest of Bernard's verses in the third canto are devoted to another hackneyed theme: episcopal luxury. He observes that ungodly men are bishops and abbots, ones not in command of themselves who are supposed to lead the way for others. To illustrate the bishop's waywardness, the poet describes his daily rounds. In the morning, His Lordship fills his useless sepulcher of a stomach with breakfast, and then sets out for the hunt:

> The upright bishop goes out for hares, goes hawking,
> The leash is removed, the wild beast sought and roused;
> A sleek horse adds to his splendor and his elegance;
> Neither Greece nor Thrace offers a better mount.

A soldier walks at his side, a companion to honor him;
By chance not a single cleric accompanies him.
Now horn blares, grove resounds, echo reverberates.
A doe along the way, punished by flight, falls into nets;
His Lordship returns late with dogs barking and leaping.
Cool darkness comes on, at night sumptuous fare is readied.
The steward pours Falernian or Mareotic wines;
The banquet is rich, the pastor reclines on lofty couch.
Food is everywhere; then and there at last he is a pastor,
His throat, crammed with food, proclaims these words true.
But his nourishing of souls takes place but once a month,
Only at burials, only at the gifts of first fruits.
Why delay? He is fed, he eats, pastor to himself, we hear.
Roasted game is served, stewards prepare wine, bakers the rest;
The aproned cook is busy, the hearth glows, all looks cheery,
The halls filled with light and crowds are gleaming.
There is glassware no less than golden vessels;
Courses here, drinks there, with disdain for the hour.
The doe is devoured, moreover, a plump bird is added;
The bird is added, the table supports a roasted fowl.
Unmixed wine flows, the bolt fastened, the poor weep aloud.
Our bishop of the belly, false in his order, is filled with feasting.
Full, he rises and returns to the pouring ladles.
There is another round of drinking, a new blessing.
With gullet unharmed and the belly's gulf intact, he pants.
He tells of vigorous deeds and describes brave hearts.
Filled with nectar, fat with feasts, he is Epicurus.
He is wearied by torturous prayers for his flock, his duke.

Late is he summoned to inner chambers and soft coverlets;
A torch and golden taper are set before him.
The maid turns down silken covers and soft bedding;
This fleshy glob, this upright disgrace snores at shame.
In the morning, the house roars, the Church's suitor enters his sanctuary,
He seeks the church, stands briefly, and soon sits down.
He concludes a pontifical sermon thundering grandly,
An asp in his breast, mind guilty, hand burdened by a precious stone.
Thence he goes before his flock; Aaron bears his crown;
A mitre adorns his head, a jewel of India his hand.

(Ad lepores probus exit Episcopus, accipitratur,
Copula solvitur, et fera quaeritur, atque citatur.
Ergo nitens equus addit ei decus, immo decorem,
Quo neque Graecia sed neque Thracia dat meliorem.
Miles obambulat ut latus excolat associatus,
Forte nec unicus est sibi clericus allateratus.
Jam tuba detonat, et nemus intonat, echo resultat;
Incidit obvia damula retia, quam fuga multat.
Sero latrantibus, exilientibus hinc repedatur,
Nox subit algida, coenaque splendida nocte paratur.
Caupo Falernica vel Mareotica vina refundit,
Coena fit afflua, pastor ad ardua fulcra recumbit.
Est cibus undique, tunc ibi denique pastor habetur,
Vera vocabula pasta cibis gula re profitetur.
Sed sua pascua non nisi menstrua sunt animarum,
Solaque funera, solaque munera primitiarum.
Quid mora? pascitur est quia dicitur, est sibi pastor.

Assa subit fera, caupo parat mera, caetera pistor,
Cinctus agit cocus, ipse nitet focus, omnia rident,
Atria lumine, nec minus agmine plena renident;
Sunt holovitrae nec minus aurea vascula coram,
Hic data fercula, sunt ibi pocula, fastus ad horam.
Damula manditur, insuper additur altile crassum,
Additur altile mensa volatile suscipit assum.
Vina fluunt mera, firmior est sera, plorat egenus;
Ventris episcopus, ordine reprobus, est dape plenus.
Surgit homo satur, ad cyathos detur inde recursus;
Fit nova potio, cui benedictio fit nova rursus.
Gutture sospite, stanteque gurgite ventris anhelat,
Gestaque strenua narrat, et ardua corda revelat.
Nectare plenior, et dape pinguior, est Epicurus.
Hac teritur cruce, pro grege pro duce vota daturus.
Ad penetralia, strataque mollia sero vocatur;
Lampas et aureus hinc sibi cereus antelocatur;
Serica pallia, fulcraque mollia vernula vertit;
Carneus hic globus, et reprobus probus ad probra stertit.
Mane fremit domus, Ecclesiae procus intrat ad Aedes,
Ecclesiam petit, ut minimum stetit, est sibi sedes.
Grande tonantia pontificalia verba perorat,
Pectoris aspide, mens rea, jaspide dextra laborat.
Inde gregem praeit, hinc Aaron vehit et diadema,
Mitra caput colit, atque manum polit Indica gemma.)

(III. 423-64)

This passage amply demonstrates Bernard of Morval's satirical skills. The precision of expression, the selection of telling details, the play on words - all combine to offer the grotesque portrait of a mitred Trimalchio. In the best satirical manner, it presents to view a type, a caricature weighed down by its own enormities. At many points in the second and third cantos, Bernard reveals this capacity to provoke in the reader a most disquieting laugh. Though his themes are rarely fresh, his inventiveness of expression and imagery rescue his work from a stilted imitation. The poet of <u>De contemptu mundi</u> marshals the <u>auctores</u> in his service; he rants in disgust, weeps in sorrow for the folly of his age. But on his face, as I see him, is also the wry smile of the satiric <u>persona</u>.

Bernard liberally employs the traditional devices of his genre. Every theme is exaggerated, every satiric description spiced with ironic wit, as in that of the bishop above. There is occasional topicality, and some indecent humor, which S. M. Jackson felt constrained to modify or suppress in offering Preble's translation to the reading public. Thus, the bold line: In Venerem ruit in coitum fluit, omnis et unus (II. 569) is rendered, "One and all rush into passion and animal indulgence."[22] The objects of Bernard's sardonic outbursts are always types, never individuals, though puns, of which he is fond, may shroud some real identities from us, if not from his contemporary audience. I have noticed, for example, that he puns several times (e.g., II. 265; 270) on <u>pons</u>, the root of <u>pontifex</u>, in suggesting that bishops at that time (<u>hoc tempore</u>) no longer act as a bridge for souls (<u>pons animarum</u>). It happens that Peter the Venerable's predecessor at Cluny was the unpopular, in fact, disgraced Pons de Melguil.[23] Though he does not explicitly identify any contemporary in the poem, Bernard often declares (nine times, in fact) that he could name names. He comes closest to doing so in describing a hypocritical monk as follows:

One of these, with ancient brow, as if more righteous,
Is a school of conduct for brothers lower in the order.
His heart ponders evils, his mouth proclaims goodness.
O shame! O wickedness! Thought an angel, he is Satan.
He is Satan in works, the very same man an angel in words;
What the sound teaches, the act of this enemy unteaches.

(Fronte vetustior, et quasi justior unus eorum
Inferioribus ordine fratribus est schola morum.
Cor mala ruminat, os bona seminat, et bona fatur,
O pudor, o scelus! Est Sathan, angelus esse putatur,
Est Sathan actibus, ipseque vocibus angelus idem,
Quod sonus edocet, actio dedocet, hostis eidem.)

(II. 735-40)

Bernard followed the Roman satirists in employing the hexameter, though in a rare form. The entire poem is constructed in dactylic hexameter with both internal and tailed rhyme, a verse form known as tripartiti dactylici caudati. Though the form has appealed to hymn writers, most critics of Bernard in recent times have labeled it boring, tedious or, in one case, haunting.[24] Bernard himself was proud of it, and attributed his ability to sustain it for so long to nothing less than the assistance of Almighty God. He remarked with some satisfaction in his letter to Peter that the difficulty of the metre had rendered it virtually obsolete in his day, noting that it had been used in the past by Hildebert of Lavardin, and, in a satire of some thirty lines, by Wilchard of Lyon.[25] The former was, I am sure, a model for our poet. Several of Hildebert's themes, phrases and verbal patterns appear in De contemptu mundi.[26] Also, I have noticed that Peter Damian, who wrote a few verses on the misery of the human condition, used Bernard's metre for a short poem petitioning the Virgin for protection from dangerous storms.[27]

Our poet exhibits a fascinating range of poetic figures and sound devices in <u>De contemptu mundi</u>. Among those to which he seems most attracted are <u>singula singulis</u>, or stringing series of words together, as in a series of verbs, followed by their subjects, followed by their objects. Sometimes he runs together rather long lists of nouns and verbs extending for several lines. He is much given to repetitions and appositions. He uses alliteration widely, sometimes for several lines running. In short, there is a remarkable poetic flexibility in the poem, though the metre itself never varies. A study of Bernard's versification would be rewarding, but since it could contribute little to a discussion of satire <u>per se</u>, I shall not undertake it here.

In the preface to his 1929 edition of <u>De contemptu mundi</u>, H. C. Hoskier indicted the "learned world" for "a gross piece of carelessness to have allowed near eight centuries to pass without popularizing Bernard of Cluny's work." He added, "I feel convinced that Bernard's poem has only to be put in its entirety in the hands of the intelligent public of today for the reading public to rise up and call him blessed."[28] Hoskier's conviction has not been borne out. Bernard remains obscure, owing undoubtedly to a number of reasons, which would surely include the length of his work, the lack of a sound translation, the redundancy of his themes. Those who do take up his poem, however, discover in its pages a rich index to twelfth-century life and letters. There is a masterful blend of the Church and the world, of divine and secular learning, all in evocative and forceful verses. If I may counterpose a view to Mr. Hoskier's, I am confident that the intelligent public of today will not read Bernard of Morval's <u>De contemptu mundi</u>; few will ever hear of it. Those who do will not regret it.

CHAPTER II

NOTES

[1]H. C. Hoskier, ed. De Contemptu mundi: A Bitter Satirical Poem of 3000 lines Upon the Morals of the XIIth Century by Bernard of Morval (London, 1929). The poem was previously published in its entirety in Thomas Wright, The Anglo-Latin Satirical Poets and Epigrammatists of the Twelfth Century, Vol. II (London, 1872).

[2]Quoted in S. M. Jackson, The Source of Jerusalem the Golden (University of Chicago Press, 1910) 45. Jackson's introduction and bibliography include detailed descriptions of the first seven editions of our poem, and he prints Henry Preble's translation of the entire work, which had appeared in the American Journal of Theology in January, April and July of 1906.

[3]Horatio W. Parker, Hora Novissima: The Rhythm of Bernard de Morlaix on the Celestial Country Set to Music for Soli, Chorus, and Orchestra (Op. 30) with English translation by Isabella G. Parker and Introduction by H. Wiley Hitchcock (Da Capo Press, New York, 1972).

[4]The Mariale ascribed to Bernard is printed in Analecta Hymnica Medii Aevi, Vol. 50. For other works attributed to him, see A. Wilmart, "Grands poémes inedits de Bernard le Clunisien," Revue Bénédictine XLV (1933) 249-54.

[5]"Nam quia inter contemporaneos meos fama bene versificandi mihi licet immerito circumvolabat, et vicia perditorum vix aliquis aut nullus viva voce nedum litterali reprehendebat, concaluit cor meum intra me."

[6]George J. Engelhardt, "The 'De contemptu mundi' of Bernardus Morvalensis, Part One: A Study in Commonplace," Mediaeval Studies 22 (1960) III. Engelhardt published his study of

Book Two in MS 26 (1964) 109-42, and Book Three in MS 29 (1967) 243-72.

[7] De miseria conditionis humanae, ed. R. Lewis (Univ. of Georgia, 1978). Conrad's Dialogus de mundi contemptu vel amore was edited by R. Bultot as number 19 in Analecta Mediaevalia Namurcensia (Louvain, 1966). A useful study of the contemptus mundi theme is Francesco Lazzari, Il Contemptus Mundi Nella Scuola Di S. Vittore (Naples, 1965).

[8] J. F. Benton, " 'Mundus Deciduus,' Possibly by Alan of Lille," Archives D'Histoire Doctrinale et Litteráire du Moyen Age XLIX (1982) 292-95.

[9] Henry's verses are in Wright, Anglo-Latin Satirists II, 171-74. For the contemptus mundi theme in his history, see the chapter "History and Contempt of the World," in Nancy Partner, Serious Entertainments: The Writing of History in Twelfth Century England (Univ. of Chicago, 1977).

[10] Jean Leclercq, The Love of Learning and the Desire for God (New York, 1974) 66-77.

[11] Charles Witke, Latin Satire: The Structure of Persuasion (Leiden, 1970) 206. Bernard's poem is classified as a "complaint" in John Peter, Complaint and Satire in Early English Literature (Oxford, 1956) 30-33 and 36-39.

[12] Hoskier, xvi.

[13] H. Keil, Grammatici Latini I, 485.

[14] David S. Wiesen, St. Jerome as a Satirist (Cornell University Press, 1964) 270.

[15] This is true of Engelhardt's study cited above. See also, Ray C. Petry, "Medieval Eschatology and Social Responsibility in Bernard of Morval's 'De Contemptu mundi'," Speculum XXIV (1949) 207-17.

[16] Harry Levin, The Myth of the Golden Age in the Renaissance (Oxford, 1969) 33.

[17] John H. Mozley and R. R. Raymo, Nigel de Longchamps Speculum Stultorum (University of Calif. Press, 1960) 6-7.

[18] Rosario Leotta, ed. Marbodo, Liber Decem Capitulorum (Rome, 1984); A. Brian Scott, Hildeberti Cen. Episcopi Carmina Minora (Leipzig, 1969). Poems attributed to Marbod and Hildebert are also printed in PL 171. "De muliere mala" is in Petri Pictoris Carmina, ed. L. Van Acker, Corpus Christianorum (Continuatio Mediaevalis) XXV (1972) 105-16.

[19] Wiesen, 148-60.

[20] Jackson, 9.

[21] John A. Yunck, The Lineage of Lady Meed: The Development of Medieval Venality Satire (University of Notre Dame, 1963) III. Later Yunck writes, "Bernard is rarely capable of moderation. His poetry lives on the extremes of emotion -- either raptures of delight or paroxysms of fury."

[22] Jackson, 142.

[23] For a detailed chapter on Pontius of Melguil, see L. M. Smith, Cluny in the Eleventh and Twelfth Centuries (London, 1930) 237-84.

[24] Samuel H. Cross, "H. C. Hoskier, ed., De contemptu mundi, by Bernard of Morval," a review in Speculum V (1930) 452.

[25] Wilchard's verses, which begin with the line, "Ordo monasticus ecclesiasticus esse solebat," were printed by Mathias Flacius Illyricus, along with Bernard's De contemptu mundi, in Varia doctorum piorumque virorum de corrupto Ecclesiae statu Poemata (Basel, 1557). In Wright, Anglo-Latin Satirists II, the poem is ascribed to Gualo the Briton under the title "Invectio in Monachos."

[26] Scott notes several parallels between the poets in the testimonia of his Hildebert edition.

[27] Margareta Lokrantz, ed. L'Opera Poetica Di S. Pier Damiani (Stockholm, 1964) 60 and 141.

[28] Hoskier, xi-xii.

CHAPTER III
HUGH OF ORLEANS

O quam dura sors Primatis!
- Hugh of Orleans -

The favorite theme of Hugh, known as the Primate (<u>Primas</u>) of Orleans, was his own misfortune.[1] Exclaimed against a background of folly and hypocrisy, his complaints seize the reader's attention. This old, misunderstood, maltreated figure vividly exposes, through his own suffering, an unjust, uncaring world. His brief collection of lyrics recites a litany of ills: poverty, senectitude, violence, rejection, even winter's winds. Ironically, Hugh's admitted depravity (drunkenness, gambling, harlotry) causes much of his distress. Often, he reiterates his lamentable condition with lines such as:

>Unlucky Primas lost five dollars
>(Infelix Primas perdidit V solidos)
>
>   (1. 26)

or,

> Poorer I live than every captive, pauper or deserter
> (Omni captivo vel paupere vel fugitivo/Pauperior vivo)
>
> (6. 11-12)

or,

> I was poor, deprived . . .
> (Pauper eram, spoliatus . . .)
>
> (18. 11)

Wretched (<u>miser</u>), poor (<u>pauper</u>), old (<u>senilis</u>) are the adjectives the poet employs to characterize his plight, and, though one is well-cautioned by Alvin Kernan against "biographical criticism," the force of personal poetry cannot be denied in the satires of Hugh.[2] He would have it so, for he names himself (<u>Primas</u>) often in the twenty-three poems of the Oxford collection. Most of these pieces are centered around a personal experience, real or imagined. Hugh's window on the world is himself. The <u>persona</u> of his poems is not an indignant onlooker, but a part of the scene. He recognizes reprobates, for he is one. He upholds the meanness of secular society and ecclesiastical circles by describing his own interactions with them. His mistakes and failed fortunes lead the reader to glimpse, through the jaded vision of a typical "wandering scholar," a world of petty foibles and rampant vice.

Little is known for certain about Hugh of Orleans, despite many citations of his name and work in the twelfth and thirteenth centuries. The fullest report appeared in the <u>Chronicon</u> of Richard of Poitiers (ca. 1170), who wrote that in 1144 or 1145, at Paris, a <u>scholasticus</u> named Hugh, worthless in character and deformed in looks, was nicknamed "Primas" by his fellow-academics.[3] The description went on to applaud his considerable education in letters, his fame for wit, knowledge, eloquence, and his talent for rhyming. Finally, Richard quoted a line of Hugh's referring to him as "Primate of Orleans." Among twelfth-century writers, Matthew of Vendôme and John of Salisbury cited Primas of Orleans, and Serlo of Wilton composed verses in his memory. Early in the thirteenth century, Thomas of Capua and Alexander Neckam mentioned Primas in their works, while Henri d'Andeli called him a champion of Grammar in his <u>Bataille des Sept Arts</u>.[4]

These numerous citations of his poetry notwithstanding, this "shadowy, will-of-the wisp rhymester" remains an enigma, and the details of his life are largely shrouded.[5] Nevertheless, we can confidently assert that he was a widely-acclaimed poet who flourished in the schools of France at sometime during the middle decades of the twelfth century. The clever lyrics which brought him fame then still have the power to amuse the modern reader and compel his admiration.

The uncommon individuality of Hugh's satire places him in the tradition of Horace, who claimed (<u>Sermones</u> II. 1.30-34) to follow the practice of Lucilius. Horace's satires abound in autobiographical details, some of which trace his affection for a noble patron and his love for a humble father, while others comically deplore the misadventures of a journey or an encounter with a clinging bore.[6] Hugh's satirical verses, though often brief and shrill, resemble the <u>sermones</u> ("conversations") of genial Horace in many ways, especially the creation of vivid scenarios, and a posture which includes worldly wisdom and self-irony.[7] Hugh is less restrained in complaint, less endearing in temperament than his Roman predecessor, but he is as much a keen-sighted realist whose revelations of his world include himself, body and soul.

Hugh, like Horace, ridiculed reprobates of high and low station in life; in clever verses he censured the unworthy bishop, the fraudulent professor, the inconstant harlot, and the deceitful host. Though various historical figures have been suggested as his objects, Hugh primarily followed the convention of mocking types rather than individuals, as is clear from his use of the common name "Flora" for the prostitute or simply <u>pontifex</u> for bishop.

Perhaps Hugh's most famous poem (#I) is his complaint against a certain red-haired host (<u>hospes rufus</u>). In this wonderfully compact, ironic piece, Hugh implicitly chides his own vices as he castigates the host who fleeced him. His opening verses clearly hint at disaster to come:

> A host had professed himself much my friend,
> promising a lot, delivering little.
> His name I won't say, if anyone inquires,
> But I'll tell what he was like: red-haired.
>
> (Hospes erat michi se plerumque professus amicum,
>   Voce michi prebens plurima, re modicum.
> Quis fuerat taceo, si quis de nomine querat;
>   Set qualis possum dicere: rufus erat.)

Hugh goes on to describe his warm reception and the host's solicitous welcome. However, this house proved full of deceit and guile (<u>fraus et dolus</u>), the host cunning (<u>astutus</u>), himself unlucky (infelix). The poet, soon drunk and drowsy, is enticed to gamble. Of course, the dice fail him, the wine keeps flowing, and his once-jingling purse grows silent. The poem concludes with a curse on such a "friend."

This poem illustrates several of Hugh's favorite satirical devices. One is to place himself at the center of turmoil: Primas outcast, Primas cheated, Primas assaulted, Primas abandoned in love. His persona, enveloped in misfortune, is the focal point of his verses. Moreover, his own failings are ironic objects of the satire, for the poet clearly suggests that he is sometimes rash and imprudent, and ever-poor. Finally, he ridiculed types who represented all the foibles of a class. Wayfarers must be ever-vigilant, for unscrupulous hosts everywhere are ready to greet them with cheerful welcome, while plying them with strong drink and stealing their money. Poem #1, then, is about the poet and the host, the one undone by naivete and folly, the other using the tricks of his trade to rob unwary guests. The poem is a classic on the fraudulent host, a popular medieval theme.[8]

Hugh Primas' satire of types included the meretrix. His "harlot poems" (#6, 7, 8) are not examples of mordant antifeminism so popular among twelfth-century monastic writers; rather, their forte depends on brilliant irony, hyperbole, word play and obscenity. In each, the poet becomes the "victim" of the grasping, faithless lady, but her wily deceits are employed against one too credulously naive.

The subject of the first such poem (#6) is Flora.[9] In a typical play-on-words, the poet reports:

> It was the season of flowers when the best of these,
> My flower, Flora, abandoned my bed . . .
>
> (Tempus erat florum cum flos meus, optimus horum,
> Liquit Flora thorum, fons fletus, causa dolorum)
> (6. 3-4)

The poet, counterpoising Flora with the verb <u>flere</u> (to weep), goes on to bewail the restless days, the sleepless nights of longing for his beloved. He weeps, and lives more wretchedly than a captive or a fugitive, while Flora, enticed by money, shares another's bed. The poem closes with the writer comparing himself to a chaste turtledove (<u>turtur</u>) and Flora to a lustful one (<u>columba</u>). This satire, in the form of a lament, attacks the harlot's inconstancy, while equally mocking the man who expects fidelity from a prostitute.

The next poem (#7) takes the form of a mock <u>consolatio</u>. Boethian in tone at the outset, it calls upon the suffering poet (Flora has left him again) to be wise, to endure, to answer a hard lot with a brave heart. It rehearses the deceits and infidelities of the harlot, who cares only for food, clothes, money. She is flattering (<u>blanda</u>), but faithless (<u>perfida</u>), and to consort with her brings ridicule and misery:

> Why do you mourn, lyric poet, why grieve for a harlot?
> Be relieved, be silent, friend, nor let sorrow sting you.
> We know -- and it is something -- that your Flora has left you.
> But never mind; many are able to speak to you
> Who in like manner, in like sorrow, have pined away.
> Sorrow for a mistress will cast you down swiftly to death

Unless you oppose a hard lot with a brave heart.
What a hard lot offers, a wise man ought to despise;
As often as there is no power to alter sad affairs,
Patience renders sorrows light for one bearing them well.
But rather, let us endure what we cannot change!
By your lyre soothe the grief conceived of wrath.
Rest a little, for I mean to tell of wonders.
Be still a little! Neither burdensome nor bitter will it be
If now we teach a man unknowing the ways of these women.
A seductress does not love a seducer without a purse.
She rejoices in a plate full of food, in a flask
Pouring wine, a meal, more than in sweet-sounding song.
When the kitchen smell reaches her nose, she delights
In tripe or some squalor more than the charm of music.
When a garment is given or a good meal is ready,
Then command what you will: then she will be ever-fawning.
But when this clinging flatterer takes your presents away,
The faithless one seeks a better man to devour and destroy.
Him once found and your gift borne away, she abandons you;
She will leave you a pauper, despised and released.
When your "thing" is diminished, the one who has her profit
Will recall neither your goods spent nor deeds well done.
While you grieve, the people's joke, the fornicator smiles,
The village will laugh, as will he and the harlot laugh.
For the mind of woman, like swift children and spring wind,
Knows not how to pity the pitiable.
Since you give nothing, a small coin's sound carries her off.
Again you promise; swift will be her return.
If your purse jingles, which gives her a little hope,

The purse counsels her return; she flies back, him rejected,
Nor does the liar dismiss a friend unless he is needy.
A purse summons an adulteress as a bird's severed leg
Or spied bits of flesh attract the sparrow-hawk.
When she has her price, then she will solemnly swear:
"I shall not forsake you unless you forsake me first."
When you have given money, she swears that you are the best;
Then will she feign tears and bestow on you her best parts;
"Though another give me more, I love you more," she says,
So that she might procure a gift and drain you entirely.
She guards her own things, unknowing how to spare yours,
Goading him who tarries; give quickly, or she hates you.
When, poor wretch, you give goods, as you hand them over,
She asks not whence they came or where you, pauper, go.

(Quid luges, lirice, quid meres pro meretrice?
Respira, retice neque te dolor urat, amice.
Scimus et est aliquid quia te tua Flora reliquit.
Set tu ne cures, possunt tibi dicere plures,
Qui simili more, simili periere dolore.
Teque dolor scorti dabit afflictum cito morti,
Ni dure sorti respondes pectore forti.
Quod mala sors prebet, sapiens contempnere debet;
Res quociens mestas non est mutare potestas,
Mesta ferendo bene reddit paciencia lene.
Set quin perferimus, quod permutare nequimus.
Consolare lyra luctum, quem parturit ira.
Paulum respira, quia destino dicere mira.
Ergo quiesce parum; nec erit grave sic nec amarum,

Si nunc ignarum mores doceamus earum.
Lenonem lena non diligit absque crumena.
Lance cibo plena, vinum fundente lagena,
Plus gaudet cena quam dulce sonante Camena.
Cum nidor naso veniet, gaudebit omaso
Aut aliqua sorde plus quam dulcedine corde.
Cum vestis danda vel erit bona cena paranda,
Tunc quidvis manda, tunc semper erit tibi blanda.
Set cum dona feret, que nunc tibi blanda coheret,
Quem voret et laceret pociorem perfida queret.
Quo semel invento te munere linquet adempto,
Cedet contempto te paupere teque redempto.
Que predam nacta, cum res fuerit tua fracta,
Tu risus plebis mecho ridente dolebis,
Risus erit ville, meretrix ridebit et ille.
Nescit enim miseris misereri mens mulieris
Mobilibus pueris ventoque simillima veris.
Quam, quia nil dederis, modici sonus auferet eris;
Promittas rursus: velox erit inde recursus.
Si tibi bursa sonet, que spem modicam sibi donet,
Bursa redire monet; revolabit eumque reponet,
Nec nisi mendicum mendax dimittit amicum.
Bursa vocat mecham, veluti vocat ad cirotecam
Crus avis excissum vel visa caruncula nisum.
Sumpto quadrante tunc iurabit tibi sancte:
"Non dimittam te, nisi me dimiseris ante."
Cum dederis nummum, iurabit te fore summum,
Tunc finget lacrimas partesque dabit tibi primas;
"Alter plura licet michi det, te plus amo" dicet,
Munus ut extricet et totum prodiga siccet.

Nam sua custodit, te nescia parcere rodit,
Tardantemque fodit; nisi des cito, quod volet, odit.
Cumque miser tua das, non querit, dum sibi tradas,
Unde hoc corradas vel egens quo denique vadas.)

In the third meretrix poem (#8), Hugh sets out, with a sardonic smile, one imagines, to define the mores of the prostitute. He contrasts her vain, disdainful behavior on a "house call," with the squalid conditions of her own meager quarters (domus exilis; casa sordida vilis). In the former situation, the adorned visitor demands extravagant preparations, which the eager client must provide:

You arrange everything splendidly -- for a whore!
(Omnia magnifice disponis pro meretrice)

(8. 12)

Of course, the harlot appreciates nothing, hardly tasting the sumptuous dishes and merely sipping the fine wines. Then, at his ironic, humorous and obscene best, the poet reports that, after all this pampering, at night she acts like a virgin! She whimpers, moans, will not cooperate, and complains of your size, this one who could take on a mule if she wanted! In the morning, she returns to a miserly existence, entertaining mimes and camp-servants in filthy stalls for a little money.

This piece by Hugh, characterized by superb irony, double-entendres and patent obscenity, is probably inspired by a brief passage in Terence's Eunuchus (lines 934-39).[10] In fact, the medieval poet borrows Terence's image of the meretrix at home dipping crusts of stale bread in warmed-over broth. However, once again the realism of misadventure dominates a poem by Hugh Primas. The prostitute's haughty bearing, the humiliating frustration she causes, her preference for ignoble drudges -- all reflect on the duped poet as much as they satirize harlotry. Apart from the satirical conventions, proverbial expressions, and verbal reminiscence of Roman authors, there remains in the meretrix poems that wry intrusion of personality which reveals High Primas grimly smiling at himself.

The Oxford verses of Hugh also include three poems (#3, 9, 10) on classical themes. These are not satires, but have all the earmarks of school exercise. They are in leonine hexameters, full of puns, and they offer rather conventional retellings of popular stories. The first (#3), which ends abruptly after fifty-two lines, recounts the descent of Orpheus into the underworld to rescue Eurydice from the realms of death. #9, of exactly the same length, laments the fall of mighty Troy, and contrasts its former splendor with the now-barren wasteland. One might view this piece, in view of such exclamations as Heu, quid agunt bella! preciosa iacent capitella (Alas, what wars do! columns of great price lie crumbled), as satire on war, but the theme of Troy in ruins certainly was a commonplace in twelfth-century literature.[11]

The third "classical" poem of Hugh, somewhat longer, is more distinctive. Inspired certainly by a satire of Horace (II. 5), it details the meeting between Ulysses and the prophet Teiresias (originating in Odyssey, bk. 11). Horace had made Homer's somber encounter an occasion for sharp humor as he used it to ridicule the legacy hunters of Rome with this counsel to the Ithacan hero: escape your penury by becoming an heir; you're clever enough; you only need become a fawning hypocrite to recoup your fortune, and be sure to make Penelope a partner in your scheme. Hugh Primas restores the serious tone to this famous meeting, and he actually shifts the main focus to the virtuous Penelope. Her long-suffering faithfulness to Ulysses becomes the basis of a <u>consolatio</u>:

> And dry your tears, while such a chaste companion lives!
> (Et lacrimas sicca, socia vivente pudica)
>
> (10. 51)

These verses (lines 23-65) <u>de muliere bona</u> markedly contrast with the misogyny of so much twelfth-century satire, where Juvenal's view that a good woman is a "rare bird on earth, like a black swan," became a favorite, indeed a proverbial expression. In fact, in this poem Hugh writes:

> Your famous lot is now neither heavy nor bitter
> While your woman, a rare bird, is poor, not greedy.
>
> (Sors tua preclara, iam nec gravis est nec amara,
> Dum sit avis rara mulier pauper nec avara)
>
> (10. 53-4)

Hugh employs Penelope's virtues to indict the vices commonly attributed to women by his contemporaries. He stresses her poverty, her sacrifices to preserve chastity:

> You will see Penelope poor, an old woman in sorrow,
> Who lives in need because she chose to be pure.

> (Penelopem cernes inopem vetulamque dolore.
> Vivit mendica, quia maluit esse pudica)
>
> (10. 23-4)

He relates her material losses directly to her rejection of promiscuity:

> If she would become an adulteress, her storeroom would not be empty.
> (Si fieret mecha, non esset inops apotheca)
>
> (10. 25)

He underscores this idea by repeating the words moecha, moechus, meretrix (adulteress, adulterer, harlot) five times between lines 25 and 31. Thus, Hugh's moralistic verses invite the reader to contrast those faithless women who surrender themselves to blandishments and treasures with the outstanding classical model of chastity, Penelope.[12]

Hugh Primas' invective was twice directed at bishops. In a brief, sarcastic poem (#11), beginning with the words Primas pontifici (Primas to the bishop), he suggests that a prelate with a reputation for high living, one who enjoys fine clothes, food and sex, should also drink well, to avoid sickness. The adverb bene (well), repeated six times in five lines, ironically emphasizes the bishop's improprieties, and might even hint at his name. The theme of worldly bishops was a favorite in medieval satire, and Hugh contributed a much longer piece (#16) to it. The 156 lines of #16 have been called "the most curious production of Hugh."[13] The poem is a mixture of topics and languages, almost one third of the verses containing Old French mingled with Latin. Essentially, this macaronic poem is a plea for provisions, and entirely consistent with the persona of Hugh's satires. He praises the city of Sens, where he received kind hospitality, including the gift of a good horse from the Archdeacon. Now he must petition the Archbishop for oats and hay. Much of #16 is given over to these topics, but its introductory verses (1-57) constitute a satire on an episcopal election and a dissolute bishop. The poet begins by expressing personal distress and a moral outrage which compel him to write:

> Moved by affronts and assaults,
> Long have I harbored too much grief.
> Now at last I must break my silence,
> Perceiving the sad humiliation of the Church,
> The cleric's dishonor and shame.
>
> (Iniuriis contumeliisque concitatus
> Iam diu concepi dolorem nimium.
> Nunc demum runpere cogor silencium,
> Cernens ecclesie triste supplicium
> Et cleri dedecus atque flagicium)
>
>   (16. 1-4)

He reproaches a city (identified in line 58 as Beauvais) for electing a monk as bishop while slighting a cleric. Ascribing the choice to envy, Hugh observes that now the cleric pays homage to this monk whom, if met on the highway, one would think a great devil (grande demonum). Then he unfolds the familiar complaints. This bishop, pale and thin from fasts, soon learned to devour sumptuous banquets, to consume streams of wine; within two years he grew fat as a hog, often carried drunk to bed. Charges of nepotism, hypocrisy, cruelty and homosexuality follow in rapid succession, and the poet completes his indictment by declaring to the city:

> Then does your madness first appear,
> When the bishop's incontinence is evident,
> His vanity and greed,
> His foolishness and ignorance.
>
> (Tunc primum apparet vestra dementia,
> Quando pontificis incontinentia
> Et vanitas patet et avaritia,
> In quibusdam folie et ignorantia)
>
> (16. 54-7)

With all respect for the several attempts to identify the bishop of #16, and without denying that Hugh might have had a particular person in mind, I am confident that his purpose in the satire is to ridicule the regular clergy as a type. From the outset of the work, he stresses the contrast between a cleric (a "brother" nourished in the bosom of the Church) and the monk (a great cowled demon), and he openly counsels that when the necessity of election arises, a cleric should be chosen. Moreover, Hugh follows this advice with the repetition of an earlier, favorable image of the cleric as the son to whom Mother Church should be entrusted. This is the dishonor and shame of the cleric, the humiliation of the Church with which the poem opens: Monks, strangers, are being elected to bishoprics, while clerics, faithful sons, are denied. The glory of Sens, which Hugh now turns to (70ff.) derives from its election of a faithful son (<u>fidelis filius</u>), not another stranger (<u>advenam alium</u>). That Archbishop of Sens, as line 82 confirms, was a cleric (<u>cleri leticiam</u>).

Two of the longer poems in the Oxford collection are #18 and 23. In the former, the poet begins with praise for Amiens, an encomium which rests principally on the city's kindness to him. Like the good Samaritan, Amiens has comforted our poet when he was poor, naked and robbed -- by dice! Thus, he reports, the city is a worthy offspring of Reims, which, by virtue of its age, holds a preeminent place among cities. The acknowledgement of Reims' venerable position leads Primas to the central theme, the celebrated school of Alberic, and a brief, but virulent attack on an unnamed teacher who discredits the academy by his scandalous ways. The school is called a fountain (fons is repeated five times) of discipline, of doctrine, not a place of trifles (nugae) or false arguments. Curiously, Primas boasts that the grammatical arts of Martianus and Priscian are not part of this education, nor are the vanities of poets. He reiterates: Non leguntur hic poete. Later he eliminates Socrates and Plato by name from the curriculum, all in favor of Saint John and the prophets. The absence of arts from a theological school is not surprising, but Primas' disparagement of those disciplines surely is. Perhaps it is a pretense for some ulterior purpose.[14] Then Primas launches a concentrated, severe attack. Several historical figures, including Abelard, have been suggested as Primas' enemy, who is called thief (fur) and robber (latro), and identified with Gnatho, the parasite of Terence's Eunuchus.[15] Whipped, branded and scarred, he is a glutton, a monk whom Primas invites to return to his cowl and dark habit. He abruptly ends with a call for the enemy's departure, silence or punishment.

The final poem (#23) in the Oxford collection is a display of contrasts. It recounts Primas' expulsion from a house, i.e., community, for coming to the defense of a lame, old brother who has also been driven out. Considerable effort has been devoted to illuminating the specific type of community from which Primas was exiled and that to which he now appeals for aid. The prevailing view is that the former was a hospital.[16] With those much-discussed questions set aside, two fascinating considerations remain: the characterization of the speaker, Primas, and the bitter attack on the enemy who banished him. The two men are cleverly contrasted. Primas, once rich, esteemed and preeminent, is now bent by old age, worn out, poor and neglected. He has been cast out (<u>deiectus</u>), driven from the house (<u>pulsus</u>), exposed to wind and rain. Worst of all, he is responsible for his own sufferings. Like a Judas, he acted imprudently and handed himself over to the betrayer when he abandoned a secure, honorable community for the one which now scorns him. He is remorseful, weeping, burdened and outcast, literally thrown in the mud. The poet employs a remarkable number of pitiful images to portray the unfortunate speaker, now victimized for his charity (<u>pro bono</u>).

Primas' object of attack is a chaplain (<u>capellanus</u>) who turned on him. The man, false and proud, faithless and wicked (<u>mendax, vanus, infidelis, profanus</u>), had fraudulently deceived our poet, while his purse was full, with expressions of love and welcome. Then the betrayer had fleeced him and thrown him out. The immediate cause of Primas' expulsion was his defense of a maltreated, lame, old brother. Thus Primas' act of Christian charity, with no one's aid but God's (<u>nemo praeter deum</u>), takes on a heroic stature, while the chaplain becomes more despicable. Further, the poet interweaves many charges of his vicious behavior: he is <u>not</u> a eunuch at night; he is the corruptor of women; he gambles away the Church's money. In short, the chaplain lacks purity, honesty, loyalty and love. However, the poet's clever irony is at work again, for he has Primas clearly reveal that his own naive lack of foresight and caution caused his problems (<u>Primas sibi non prospexit, neque dolos intellexit</u>). He states plainly that he was deceived by flattery (<u>hoc deceptus blandimento</u>) and cheated (<u>emunctus sum argento</u>). Since he includes gambling among the chaplain's vices, and we know that Primas was addicted to it, we understand more clearly that his roll in the mud for a brother's sake also had something to do with the roll of the dice! Again, the satirical barb is two-pronged; it jabs the vicious chaplain and the unwary Primas himself.

Another poem by Primas (#15) bears noteworthy resemblance to the piece we have just considered. Again, a violent rejection of Primas is the main theme. In this encounter, the poet has approached a creditor for payment due, a request answered by a frightful outburst of temper. In fact, the enraged (<u>infensus</u>) debtor, out of his mind with anger (<u>vir insanus extra sensum</u>), furiously chases Primas, who barely escapes, racing away on winged feet amidst visions of death and crying "alas." Now he hails noble Paris, queen of cities, for receiving an unfortunate exile. As in #23, there is implicit appeal for aid, the depiction of Primas as old and infirm, and the portrayal of the enemy as a deceitful flatterer turned wild. Primas, old and near death (<u>senex moriturus</u>), is identified with Zacheus, the man of small stature in Luke's gospel. Of course, in achievement he is grand: <u>Primas</u>, our good poet, master (<u>noster bonus vates; magister</u>). The creditor, by contrast, is impious, hard-hearted, a murderer, persecutor, tyrant. Gigantic in stature (<u>velut Briareus</u>), he perpetrates a monstrous crime against a defenseless victim.

This poem, then, similar as it is to #23, enables us to illustrate further the consistent persona of Primas (aged, sickly, etc.), the vagantenlieder appeal for aid, and the baseness of the satirist's enemy -- all favorite themes of our poet. The verses also offer an opportunity to observe Primas' clever blending of classical and biblical references. He contrasts the small Zacheus and the giant Briareus; he consigns his enemy to Stygian flames, along with Judas Iscariot. Also, the poem nicely displays Primas' skill with metre. For example, he begins with hexameters, but soon shifts to a sequence measure to complete the tale. This unusual combination underscores, I believe, other ironic juxtapositions in the poem. The hexameter heralds classical grandeur, while the sequence rhythms invoke the popular and ecclesiastical. The one suggests epic stature, and even echoes Vergil's Aeneid (cf. 1. 199; 2. 37; 5. 854). The other calls to mind hymns of praise to martyrs, as in Prudentius' Peristephanon, the likely source for the name "Dacianus" (the persecutor of Saint Vincent), twice-used by Primas for his own enemies (15. 47; 23. 16). Thus, our poet envelops his abrupt rejection in the high seriousness of epic metre and language, and, at the same time, lends it the overtones of sacred song. The result is delightful parody.[17]

The remaining works in the Oxford collection are a miscellany of short poems. One (#5) retells in fourteen lines the familiar narrative of the rich man and Lazarus (Luke, 16). The retributive justice of this tale, along with its minatory address to the rich and its solace for the poor, made it a favorite of preachers and moralistic versifiers. One finds it, for example, set out at length in Bernard of Morval's De contemptu mundi (l. 665ff.). Poem #4 expresses, in the context of concern for a traveler-friend, the poet's fear of the sea. This little masterpiece of sixteen verses in leonine rhymes, with its images of wind and ocean heightened by alliteration (e.g., flare in lines 1, 4, 5, and mare in 6, 7, 8, 10) wonderfully conveys the dangers of seafaring. Of course, the poet's wry humor is here too:

> Not land's way, but waterways terrify me.
> "Why does the sea scare thee?" Because the sea does not well bear me!
>
> (Non via terrarum, set me via terret aquarum.
> "Cur mare te terret?" Quia me mare non bene ferret.)
> (4. 9-10)

Again we find the poet exposing his own apprehensions in a gentle self-mockery so reminiscent of Horace.[18]

Hugh also composed epigrams, ten of which are among the Oxford poems. Some have a sexual theme (e.g., #17 and 22), while others request gifts (#21) or humorously suggest that water and wine do not mix (#14). Five of these shorter poems (#12, 13b, 19, 20a, 20b) involve a cloak or mantle (chlamys; mantellus). Mostly they complain that the cloak is unlined, cheap, full of fleas. A longer effort (twenty-three lines) on the cloak is #2. This clever piece opens with curses upon the bishop who gave a worthless present:

> Scum of bishops, filthy cleric, unclean sore,
> Who gave to me in winter an unlined cloak!

> (Pontificum spuma, fex cleri, sordida struma,
> Qui dedit in bruma michi mantellum sine pluma!)
>
> (2. 1-2)

After remarking on the snow, the ice, the thinness of the garment, Primas addresses the bishop's gift, pleading that the cloak ward off winter's blasts. The <u>mantellus</u> acknowledges its own lightness, its inability to hinder the biting Northwind without a thick lining. The cloak tells the shivering poet to buy some hides to patch the garment's holes, and then it might keep out the cold. I am compassionate and would do your bidding, affirms the cloak, but I am Jacob, not Esau.[19]

    This short satire on the stinginess of a bishop (<u>presul</u>) is certainly typical of Hugh Primas, and may serve to conclude this short essay on the nature of his work. He places himself in a position of unfortunate disadvantage, assumes a posture of righteous outrage, but hints at self-deprecation. His self-pity is redeemed by learned wit. His lonely, raucous voice still indicts folly and meanness with exceptional power.

CHAPTER THREE

NOTES

[1] The satires of Hugh Primas of Orleans are among twenty-three poems discovered in a twelfth or early thirteenth century manuscript (Rawlinson G. 109R) in the Bodleian Library at Oxford. This "Oxford collection" was published by Wilhelm Meyer, Die Oxforder Gedichte des Primas (Berlin, 1907; repr. Darmstadt, 1970). This edition is now replaced by C. J. McDonough, The Oxford Poems of Hugh Primas and the Arundel Lyrics (Toronto, 1984). Four poems are printed, with English translation, by G. F. Whicher, The Goliard Poets (New York, 1965), and #7, which I translate in this essay, was translated into English by E. H. Zeydel, Vagabond Verse (Detroit, 1966) 236-40.

[2] Alvin Kernan, The Cankered Muse (New Haven, 1959), 14-30. See McDonough, 4.

[3] The pertinent lines are printed and discussed by F. Cairns, "The Addition to the 'Chronica' of Richard of Poitiers and Hugo Primas of Orleans," Mittellateinisches Jahrbuch 19 (1984) 159-61. Cairns is suspicious of this testimony. In a compelling study, another scholar cautions us against such pseudonyms as "Primas," "Archipoeta," "Golias," and "Gauterus." See A. G. Rigg, "Golias and other Pseudonyms," Studi Medievali Series 3, No. 18 (January, 1977) 65-109.

[4] Rigg, 74-76.

[5] The quotation is from B. Marti, "Hugh Primas and Arnulf of Orleans," Speculum 30 (1955) 233.

[6] On autobiography in Horace's poetry, see pages 10-15 of D. R. Shackleton-Bailey, Profile of Horace (Cambridge, Ma., 1982). The standard survey of the satires is Niall Rudd, The Satires of Horace (Cambridge, 1966).

[7] Horace's satirical *persona* is traced by W. S. Anderson, "The Roman Socrates: Horace and his Satires," in *Satire*, ed. J. P. Sullivan (Bloomington, Ind., 1968) 1-37.

[8] For example, John of Salisbury devoted a passage to the theme in his *Entheticus*. See R. E. Pepin, "The Entheticus of John of Salisbury: A Critical Text," *Traditio* XXXI (1975) 184-87.

[9] "Flora" appears as a harlot's name in Juvenal (2. 49) and John of Salisbury's *Entheticus* (line 1337).

[10] McDonough, 7.

[11] A. Boutemy, "Le Poeme Pergama flere volo . . . et ses imitateurs du XIIe siecle," *Latomus* 6 (1946) 233-44.

[12] R. E. Pepin, "Ulysses in the Twelfth Century," *The Classical Bulletin* 62 (Spring, 1986) 28-31.

[13] Charles Witke, *Latin Satire: The Structure of Persuasion* (Leiden, 1970) 214. The poem and its central figures are discussed by C. J. McDonough, "Hugh Primas and the Bishop of Beauvais," *Mediaeval Studies* XLV (1983) 399-409.

[14] J. R. Williams, "The Cathedral School of Reims in the Time of Master Alberic, 1118-1136," *Traditio* XX (1964) 98.

[15] Witke discusses #18 in his chapter on Hugh and agrees with Meyer in identifying the villain as Abelard. The poem's complexity is richly illuminated by C. J. McDonough, "Hugh Primas 18: A Poetic Glosula on Amiens, Reims, and Peter Abelard," *Speculum* 61 (October, 1986) 806-35.

[16] A fine study of the poem and its questionable sites is C. J. McDonough, "Two Poems of Hugh Primas Reconsidered: 18 and 23," *Traditio* XXXIX (1983) 115-34.

[17] I disagree with Charles Witke, who concluded that #15 does not parody a sequence.

[18] In a famous ode (I. 3), Horace prays for the safety of the ship which bears his illustrious friend, Vergil.

[19] The "mantle poems" of Hugh were studied by T. Latzke in two articles published in *Mittellateinisches Jahrbuch*: "Die

Mantelgedichte des Primas Hugo von Orleans und Martial," 5 (1968) 54-8 and "Der Topos Mantelgedicht," 6 (1970) 109-31.

CHAPTER IV

WALTER OF CHATILLON

Rodo pravos in aperto
- Walter of Chatillon -

Among many images invoked by authors and critics to define satire, such as mirror, medicine or scourge, that of stinging or biting has become commonplace. "Biting satire" best describes the brief corpus of Walter of Chatillon,[1] for he conceived of his own invective in violent terms:

> Abbots, bishops, deacons I scourge,
> With satirical bites and tongue I lash.
>
> (Abbates, pontifices, decanos flagello
> Morsibus satiricis et lingue flagello)
>
> (13. 3.4-5)

One of his Menippean satires (3.23.1-3) acknowledges his own biting satire (<u>mordaci satira</u>), while another poem reports the imagined response of his victim in these terms:

> Shamefully do you bite us,
> For you are a sick physician and baser than all.
>
> (Turpiter nos mordes,
> Cum sis eger medicus, cum plus cunctis sordes)
>
> (7a. 13.1-2)

Among Walter of Chatillon's other images for his satirical <u>persona</u> are the sword (<u>quasi gladius</u>), whirlwind (<u>ventus turbinis</u>) and soldier (<u>bella michi video</u> . . . <u>signa tuli</u>), and once he concluded a poem with the words:

> Now let my satire put an end to its strife.
> (Iam satira faciat finem sue litis)
>
> (13. 15.4)

Walter's aggressive satire was sparked by Juvenalian indignation over vices, not Horatian foibles. He viewed his objects, especially the higher clergy, as gluttons, thieves, and instruments of pain. He referred to grasping prelates as thorns and thistles (<u>spinae et tribuli</u>), dogs (<u>canes</u>) and bulls (<u>tauri</u>); they were men who lie in wait to plunder the poor.[2] For these abusers of power, Walter reserved his most scathing expressions, and his reader cannot fail to sense the disgust of the poet toward dishonorable churchmen.

Walter was born about 1135 at Lille. Thus, John of Salisbury, who wrote to him in most affectionate terms, addressed him as Galterus ab Insula.[3] After studies at Paris and Reims, he became master of a school at Laon. Like John of Salisbury, he left the academic career in favor of an administrative post. During this period of service to Henry II, Walter was undoubtedly a member of the famous literary coterie associated with the English court.[4] At some time after the murder of Archbishop Becket in 1170, and perhaps in revulsion over it, he resumed his scholarly pursuits, teaching at Chatillon, later reading law at Bologna. In 1176, Walter accepted a position as secretary to the Archbishop of Reims. He died, a victim of leprosy, probably at Amiens. His magnum opus, completed in 1181, is an epic entitled Alexandreis.[5] However, this learned imitation of Vergil has earned small praise (and considerable criticism) from scholars, while his satires have been highly esteemed.[6]

Walter was an erudite cleric writing for educated people. His satirical themes, therefore, quite naturally address the deepest concerns of his own class: moral decay within the Church, especially avarice in the Roman Curia; the decline of letters; the plight of poor scholars. Likening himself to the "voice of one crying in the wilderness," the poet outlined these themes in the verses which his editor placed at the outset of the satirical collection. Employing this desert imagery, Walter remarks that prelates, who formerly sowed little blossoms (flosculos) of generosity and modesty, now produce only thorns and thistles. He goes on to declare that no one flourishes in this worldly wasteland unless his purse is full. This leads him to contrast prosperous flatterers and pimps with poor scholars who have neither security nor honor from their knowledge:

> What does knowledge confer on me, if, knowing, I starve?
> (Quid hoc scire michi confert/ Si sciens esurio?)
> (1. 17.5-6)

One of satire's enduring themes is the decline of literary culture, which Walter of Chatillon assails intensely. For him, study of the <u>auctores</u> had resulted in no financial benefit, but had led only to poverty. As Witke insightfully suggested, the ascendancy of the logic-choppers, John of Salisbury's "Cornificians," who promised success without wide reading, was rendering obsolete the traditional education of men like Walter.[7] Thus, his ironic verses on the decline of letters, surely inspired by cultural idealism, are based also on personal disappointment.

From the brief surviving collection of Walter's satirical poems one may glean many lines which bitterly score the world's slight estimation of learning and its unkind disregard for scholars. He often contrasts the honored position of the doctors of old (<u>antiquitus</u>) with the "modern" preference for possessors of gold, and he warns:

> Though you come accompanied by the Muses,
> You will be cast out, Homer, if you lack money!
>
> (Nam si nummo careas, foras expellere,
> Ipse licet venias musis comitatus, Homere)[8]

Walter, himself an epic poet, was horrified at the travesty of destitute poets and scholars; his heroes are the poor giants of the past: Socrates and Diogenes. Often the reader senses that Walter's rueful verses spring from keen resentment, as when he writes:

Now the band of poets wretchedly begs;
to have been steeped in literature's fount benefits no one.

(Iam mendicat misere chorus poetarum,
nulli prodest imbui fonte litterarum)

(9. 8.1-2)

More than once he alludes to the wearying hardships of study for the sole reward of penury. He frequently invokes the dark image of studious vigil (e.g., <u>cur noctis vigilias consumis</u>?; <u>vanum est scholaribus ante lucem surgere</u>) among the fruitless sacrifices of scholars who must yield to unlettered boors with fat purses. If critics have observed in Walter of Chatillon a "bitterness and fatality . . . an ironic insolence born of despair,"[9] this surely suggests his affinity to Juvenal, who, centuries before, had fueled his indignation with personal (and class) motives.[10]

Avarice, for Walter of Chatillon, was the deadliest sin. This <u>fons iniquitatis</u> was responsible for the debasement of literary education, for the demise of generosity, for simony and nepotism in the Church. Greed and its attendant corruption of Church offices is Walter's most pervasive theme. In almost every poem of the moral-satirical collection, he scores the grasping avarice of bishops, cardinals, deacons, even the doorkeepers (<u>janitores</u>) of the Church. The bishops are Pharisees, cardinals are pirates, and all, following the leprous Giezi, thirst for gold (<u>omnes aurum sitiunt</u>).[11]

The primary locus of avaricious corruption was Rome, whose fallen grandeur might inspire a rare, touching tribute in the Middle Ages, but whose moral decadence sparked countless satires.[12] In his famous poem on the city, Walter likens Rome to the perilous sea. There one must escape the voracious depths, Scylla and Charybdis, the Syrtes and the Sirens, monsters who symbolize the unremitting avarice of the Curia. The entire piece employs the imagery of the ocean and its mythological figures. Of this sea, writes Walter, Thetis is not the goddess, but Purse, mater sterlingorum . . . soror loculorum ("mother of filth-lickers, sister of coffers"). There Crassus (a name derived from crassus = fat), like a whirlpool, swallows down the world's gold and silver. In this somber poem, Walter has identified with Rome all the frightful dangers of a sea on which he had once suffered:

> But lest I happen to be shipwrecked again on this sea,
> I make an end of my words.
>
> (Set ne rursus in hoc mari/me contingat naufragari,
> dictis finem faciam)
>
> (2. 30.1-3)

Walter's verses are rich in symbols of Avarice: coins (nummi), bribes (munera), money, (pecunia), coffers (archae) and wallets (bursae). He depicts its victims as heaping up treasures (thesauros coacervant), or stuffed with riches, still gaping at more (referti spoliis . . . inhiant). They suffer from dropsy, increasing their thirst amidst abundant possessions. Furthermore, Avarice banishes generosity (largitas longe relegatur), destroys virtue and leads to vice. No one escapes its destructive power:

> The old are infected by the poison of greed,
> to boys the smell of profit is sweeter than honey;

all girls learn this before A and B:
to wish for money, not modesty.

(Senes avaritie sunt imbuti felle,
Odor lucri pueris dulcior est melle;
Nolle pudicitiam, nummos autem velle,
Hoc omnes discunt ante alpha et beta puelle)

(4. 23.1-4)

The annual Bakelfest (Feast of the Staff) offered Walter an occasion to link the themes of avarice and the demise of generosity. This "Feast of Fools," originating in France during the twelfth century, was celebrated in the Christmas season, often on January 1. For one day the liturgical order was given over to the lower clergy whose leader bore a rod or staff as symbol of office. The inversion of authority, of course, allowed the comedy of misrule, parody and revelry, and license to ridicule superiors.[13] The feast also was an occasion for gift giving. Walter was clearly attracted to Bakelfest, for it serves as the setting for several satirical poems (#1, 4, 12, 13). In these pieces he assails greedy gluttons (leccatores), while imploring the staff (baculus) to restore honesty (probitas) and generosity (largitas) to the Church. In #12 he allegorizes the staff of Moses and several other Old Testament stories in which wood is a powerful vehicle of God's power. He suggests that the baculus too must dry up the sea of avarice (fluctus avaritiae) and sweeten the waters of generosity. Again in #12 he invites the staff-bearer (baculifer) to avoid greed and to celebrate the joyous day with gifts.

Though Walter of Chatillon's main satirical themes were avarice, the decline of letters, and corruption among the clergy, his small collection of verses assails moral decay on other fronts as well. In a poem replete with Juvenalian quotations, Walter wrote:

> When I see reprobates rich with goods,
> vices rule while virtues surrender,
> women cheapened and men marry men,
> it is hard not to write satire!
>
> (Cum videam reprobos opibus affluere,
> dominari vitia, virtutes succumbere,
> vilipendi feminas, viros autem nubere,
> difficile nobis est satiram non scribere)
>
> (4. 4.1-4)

He often upholds to view this topsy-turvy world, a common medieval topos, where aberrations abound.[14] "Many-shaped are the deceits and injustices of men" (Multiformis hominum fraus et iniustitia), Walter declared, and his verses offer a clear, if swift, glimpse of most.

The papal schism (1159-1178) scandalized Walter, who devoted two poems (#7, 15) to it. He supported Alexander III against the claims of the anti-popes: Victor IV (d. 1164); Paschal III (d. 1168); Calixtus III (d. 1178). Writing sometime after the death of the latter, Walter likened Alexander III to the heroic Macedonian conqueror who would dominate his Alexandreis. King Frederick, the promoter of schism, "who presumed to set a shepherd over Zion," is called Darius; the false popes are anti-Christs. The king is warned in Walter's verses that

> Caesar has a sword, but material,
> the Pope has the same, but spiritual;
> Caesar, thus, receives temporal uses
> from him who possesses the pastoral care.
>
> (Cesar habet gladium, set materialem,
> hunc eundem pontifex, set spiritualem;
> Cesar ergo suscipit usum temporalem
> ab eo, qui possidet curam pastoralem.)
>
> (15. 15.1-4)

Thus, Walter added his voice to those raised in the conflict between papal and royal authority which was to intensify during the twelfth century. He became a faithful partisan of the ecclesiastical position, and warned bluntly in one of the schism poems:

> The Pope must not be appointed by Caesar,
> but he must be elected according to the canons.
>
> (Non erat a Cesare papa statuendus,
> sed secundum canones erat eligendus)
>
> (7. 11.1-2)

Walter's verses are sharp and witty, yet they lack many characteristic devices of the satirical genre. There are no clever Horatian scenarios, few intrusions of the author's personality, and dialogue is limited. Obscenity is rare, as are vernacular language, direct quotations and proper names, except in citations of the <u>auctores</u>.

Walter's versification is distinctive in that he abandoned the hexameter of Horace, Persius and Juvenal in favor of novel rhythmic forms. He invented the "goliardic" verse (vagantenstrophe, or "wanderer's measure") with an appended tag from classical poetry or Scripture. For example, consider:

> When I observe the world sunk in filthy stream
> and Nature's order utterly overthrown,
> and this from princes to paupers spread,
> if Nature refuses, indignation makes my verse.
>
> (Cum mundum intuear sordis fluxu mersum
> et nature penitus ordinem perversum
> et hunc a principibus in vulgus dispersum:
> si Natura negat, facit indignatio versum)
>
> (5. 4.1-4)

The closing line is borrowed directly from Juvenal's familiar first satire. These quotations, or sententiae, were known as "authorities." They epitomized a stanza and created (and maintained) a tone within the entire poem. Moreover, these allusions were intended to appeal to Walter's learned audience, in the manner of Persius and, in his own day, John of Salisbury.[15] The "authorities" most cited were the ancient satirists and Ovid, whose Ars Amatoria and Remedia Amoris seem to have placed him in the satiric tradition. Juvenal was surely Walter's favorite source. In the fourth poem, for example, the "authority" in more than half (19) of the thirty stanzas is Juvenal, who is even cited by name. Other popular Roman writers, such as Lucan, Vergil, and Cicero, occur less frequently than Horace, Persius and Juvenal, but Walter's poetry testifies to his considerable education in grammar. In some poems sharply focused on the Church, e.g. #8, Walter concluded the stanzas with Scriptural quotations rather than classical ones. Most commonly these lines were taken from the Psalms, but the Gospels, Epistles and several Old Testament books are represented. Thus, the reader of Walter's satire had to be ever alert to ancient sources which, turned to his own purposes, lent authority to the poet's invective.

In addition to novel verse forms and extensive reliance on classical/Scriptural allusions, Walter of Chatillon betrays a fondness for several other devices, including irony, allegory and puns. His clever irony has been amply described by Witke.[16] Play on words was a humorous technique of great popularity in the Middle Ages, and Walter was particularly attracted to it. The subtle force of his puns is lost in translation; most are etymological and alliterative, as in his play on pascere (to feed, nourish), whose point is that "pastors" do not nourish others, but feed themselves:

> Since they do not feed, but are fed,
> not from "I feed" are they derived,
> but from "I am fed, you are fed,"
>
> (Cum non pascant, set pascantur,
> non a "pasco" derivantur,
> set a "pascor, pasceris.")

(1. 8.4-6)

Again, "cardinals" is derived from dii carnales (gods of the flesh), while at Rome no one is pleasing (gratus) for nothing (gratis), nor is good judgment given (<u>datur</u>) without gifts (<u>datis</u>). Sometimes the puns involve proper names, as when Walter notes that Pope Alexander III was able to overcome Victor (<u>vincere Victorem</u>), and that Calixtus drained the chalice of death (<u>calicem Calixtus</u>).[17]

Allegory was extremely popular in the twelfth century, especially among the Chartrian Platonists whose favorite authors were Boethius, Macrobius, Martianus Capella and Fulgentius. Writers such as William of Conches, Bernardus Silvestris, and Walter's antagonistic compatriot, Alan of Lille, composed important philosophical allegories; theologians expounded the veiled meanings (<u>involucra</u>) of Scripture. As Wetherbee has pointed out, "It was a commonplace in the twelfth-century schools that the <u>auctores</u> had used <u>involucra</u> of imagery to veil their most profound utterances from the eyes of the ignorant and profane."[18] Walter of Chatillon's moral and satirical verses testify to his fondness for allegorical interpretation. Technical terms of allegory, such as <u>figurare</u>, <u>designare</u>, and <u>mysteria</u> appear in over half the poems, and Walter frequently offers an explanation (<u>expositio</u>) of the hidden sense beneath "the letter." In one reference to Scripture he declared:

> But if you wish to suck to the very marrow of the letter,
> you will find balsam and the honey of the Holy Spirit.
>
> (Set si velis litteram sugere medullitus,
> balsamum reperies et mel sancti spiritus)
>
> (3. 26.3-4)

Allegorical interpretations are generously laced throughout the collection of Walter's poems, especially in those composed for the Bakelfest, but they are usually concise, not sustained. One exception is #14, an allegory of the rose. Walter begins with highly allusive and laudatory verses hailing the city of Besancon, the Pope, and France, to which the rose is dedicated.[19] Then he unfolds an elaborate allegory in which the precious matter of the rose signifies wisdom, while its red color stands for charity, sister of generosity. Walter's main theme, avarice, and its opposing virtue, generosity, soon become clear. However, the poet goes on in eight stanzas (12-19) to trace deeper significations. The matter of the rose is also Christ, the Wisdom of God; the red color of the rose, too, is Christ, whose blood was spattered upon the cross. The poem concludes with a prayer that the avaricious may be sprinkled with the balm which flows from the rose to heal all wounds.

Walter of Chatillon was a moralist, a satirist, and a versatile poet. He employed his talents and wide erudition to score the moral decay of society, especially as it manifested itself in the Church he loved and served. His disgust over such decadence prompted a poem whose theme is that the way is prepared <u>now</u> for Antichrist's arrival. The introductory stanzas describe the sadly-contemplative poet observing society's ills, when, suddenly, he is transported to a dreadful vision of demons. Here the Furies, Alecto and Tisiphone, summon Antichrist to make his appearance in the corrupt world which awaits him. The satire ends with Antichrist's charge to his accomplices to go forth into every corner of the world; he pledges to follow:

While I contemplate the temper of the times,
the joys of the wicked, the sorrow of the upright,
the contempt for justice, the inactivity of faith,
I believe that the age has no ruler.

O you who bid matter to be fourfold fashioned,
who so unite unlike things in equal bond
that they are unable to be divided,
why do you allow men to be so disjointed?

Although you join the elements by definite ways
and unending laws, and set apart their strife,
it seems that man alone you reject,
whose life you do not guide with like concern.

While I wrote this with senses intent,
while I spoke of the world and its monsters,
wholly absorbed in sobs and in moans,
the spirit seized me in an ecstacy of mind.

Thinking of centaurs and the offspring of giants,
while oppressed by a great weight of cares,
I heard with cymbals and jingling of bell
demons gather from east to west.

The place where I saw the Furies gather
seemed entirely to swarm with worms
and to produce from infernal regions all the plagues
which Night begets as oft as she is disposed to copulate.

The three-headed guardian of the dead was present,
and the triad of sisters, doleful monsters,
who defile the entire assembly with gore,
and the places resound with serpents' hissing.

But neither was the source of pride absent,
who will divide the age with the sword of speech,
the son of vileness and ruin about whom
the vessel of election openly speaks.

Therefore, standing before all with excited mien,
he disdains to await the fates longer,
whence, like thunder when the cloud is scattered,
his voice bursting from his throat, so he spoke:

"Father! what delay now keeps me from being born?
Fate, why do you prevent my coming into the world?
Open the gates, but if you keep me back,
by god Beelzebub I shall go over a wall.

Now have all the signs of judgment arrived,
now the schism has come, the laws have perished,
hunger, plagues, wars have burst forth,
the dead have excessively defamed their own Anointed One.

Pitifully do I bewail the wretched Hebrews
who confess themselves mine in word and deed;
they await me, that I might come and lead
them back, and again restore Judea to the Jews.

Alecto, come forth, leave our halls,
that you might sow discord, defile covenants,
preach excess, pervert the chaste:
thus Christ will find no co-heirs."

Violently roused by these words, Alecto raged,
provoked against herself by pangs of wrath;
and so, for fury spewing madness, long-rolling
her eyes, at last she begins so:

"O grace and glory of devils, Antichrist,
O shame! What great strife, what uproar this?
Princes, who harshly devote themselves to villainy,
are your forerunners and your preachers.

Why do you seek another herald for yourself
than that false ruler of Britain who,
with triple sword, against law and custom,
shamelessly cut down the flower of priests?

What crime do you say was in Sinon?
Why do you disturb Nero over his strife?
The king who, in treachery, destroys a bishop
is truly more Neronian than Nero himself.

This alone was hateful to us about the bishop,
that his martyr's head was cut off, since the man
we know to have died for justice,
has merited paradise for himself."

When her sister's thundering was heard,
Tisiphone, girt with veil of grief and dread,
and crusted gore about her gaping mouth,
vomited forth what she had conceived in mind.

And so while a snaky army hissed, while
it crawled about her hair and face,
when she filled her breast with fury,
she began to rave with this bolt of words:

"One to whom it is allowed to torment guilty souls,
how long will people call you feeble?
Since Virtue is abolished, fallen, gone begging,
there is no one who uproots the plants of Vice.

Behold! all things lie under your sway,
the bad grows worse, the good are corrupted, bishops prone to error, with their subjects, are the forerunners of your incarnation.

In the Church you see nothing fixed,
among pastors you see Giezi's offense,
the head of the world you see weakened by schism,
and you see the papacy much decreased.

You have known well Frederick the king,
through whom you have sown seeds of schism;
therefore, you command a divided people:
who will be a better forerunner of Antichrist!

These are the ones through whom I bid every sin
to be devised, judges of others, perverters of
themselves, likened to mud and the filthy sow,
I make their arrival herald your coming."

Aroused by these quarrels, excited by the uproar
of sisterly strife, the wild mind of Pluto,
although savage and a source of discord,
yet ended the contention with well-ordered words:

"Woe, inflexible clan, woe gloomy darkness,
why do you argue among yourselves about mysteries?
To me alone is the truth exposed, made clear,
to me alone is the number of days known.

Look, the days arrive in which I become a man,
that I might overcome Enoch and Elias in wonders;
when I shall have removed Truth's way from the lands,
Rachel will serve me; I will blind Leah.

Mine are the convents, mine the cloisters,
mine are the schools, mine the monks,
mine are the kings' sceptres, mine the cardinals,
through whom I put prices on the Church's things.

Go, my confederates, go, gods of the nations,
Go, disperse throughout the crooked ways of the world;
Made flesh I shall follow you, for so have I pledged."
But these, groaning, hasten away.

(Dum contemplor animo seculi tenorem,
reproborum gaudia, proborum merorem,
contemptum iustitie, fidei torporem,
credo, quod non habeant secula rectorem.

O qui quadrupliciter ylem figurari
iubes, quo res dispares ita nexu pari
comparas, ut nequeant a se disparari:
cur permittis hominem sic denaturari?

Cum per certas methodos et leges eternas
elementa copules litemque discernas,
videtur, quod hominem solum modo spernas,
cuius vitam simili cura non gubernas.

Hoc dum mecum scriberem sensibus attentis,
dum de mundo loquerer eiusque portentis,
totus in singultibus, totus in lamentis,
rapuit me spiritus in excessu mentis.

De centauris cogitans et gigantum prole,
dum curarum premerer ponderosa mole,
audivi cum cimbalis et tinnitu nole
convenire demones ab utroque sole.

Locus, ad quem furias vidi convenire,
videbatur vermibus totus scaturire
et pestes ab inferis omnes ebullire,
quas nox gignit, quotiens libuit coire.

Affuit tergeminus ianitor silentum
et sororum trinitas, flebile portentum,
que totum commaculant sanie conventum,
et loca remugiunt sibilo serpentum.

Set nec ille defuit fons elationis,
nequitie filius et perditionis,
qui secabit seculum gladio sermonis,
de quo palam loquitur vas electionis.

Cunctis ergo facie preminens armata
indignatur amplius expectare fata,
unde quasi tonitrus nube dissipata
vox erumpens gutture sic est interfata:

"Pape! que iam mora me tenet nasciturum?
Fatum, quid me detines seculo venturum?
Pando fores, quod si me tenes exiturum,
in deo Beelzebub transgrediar murum.

Iam signa iudicii cuncta contigerunt,
iam venit discessio, iura perierunt,
fames, pestilentie, bella tumuerunt,
Christum suum inferi nimis distulerunt.

Miseranter miseror miseros Hebreos,
qui verbis et opere se fatentur meos;
expectant, ut veniam et reducam eos
et rursus restituam Iudea Iudeos.

Alecto progredere, linque nostras edes,
ut seras discordiam, federa defedes,
predices luxuriam, castos ganimedes:
sic nullos inveniet Christus coheredes."

His Alecto vocibus graviter excita
fremit ire stimulis in se lacessita;
igitur pre rabie vomens aconita,
diu torquens oculos tandem cepit ita:

'O decus et demonum decor, Antichriste,
proch pudor! que tanta lis? quis tumultus iste?
Principes, qui facinus operantur triste,
tui precursores sunt et evangeliste.

Utquid queris alium tibi precursorem
quam illum Britannie reprobum rectorem,
qui triplici gladio contra ius et morem
inpudenter messuit sacerdotum florem?

Quod fuisse facinus dicis in Sinone?
quid Neronem ventilas de seditione?
rex, qui perdit presulem in proditione,
re vera neronior est ipso Nerone.

Hoc solum de presule nobis est invisum,
quod ei martirio caput est abscisum;
nam quem pro iustitia novimus occisum,
meruisse potuit sibi paradisum".

Audito Tesiphone tonitru sororis
precincta velamine luctus et horroris,
desiccata sanie circa rictus oris,
quod mente conceperat, eructavit foris.

Igitur dum legio serpentina strepit,
dum circa cesariem et in ora repit,
ubi toto pectore furias concepit,
hoc verborum fulmine debachari cepit.

"O cui sontes animas cruciare licet,
usquequo te populus inpotentem dicet?
Cum virtus extincta sit, iaceat, mendicet,
iam non est, qui vitii plantas eradicet.

Ecce cuncta subiacent tue dicioni,
peiorantur reprobi, depravantur boni,
prelati cum subditis in errorem proni
precursores tue sunt incarnationi.

Vides in ecclesia nichil esse ratum,
vides in pastoribus Giezi reatum;
caput mundi scismate vides infirmatum,
vides et pluraliter papam declinatum.

Federicum cesarem optime novisti,
illum, per quem scismatis semina sevisti;
idcirco scismatice genti prefecisti:
quis precursor melius fiet Antichristi?

Hi sunt, per quos iubeo nefas omne strui,
aliorum iudices, perversores sui,
luto comparabiles et inmunde sui,
hos adventus facio precursores tui."

His commota litibus mens effrena Ditis,
turbata sororie pre tumultu litis,
licet fons discordie, licet sit inmitis,
litem tamen terminat verbis expolitis:

"Heu, gens inplacabilis, heu chaos austerum,
quid ad vos disserere de secretis rerum?
Michi soli panditur, michi patet verum,
michi soli cognitus numerus dierum.

Ecce dies veniunt, quibus homo fiam,
ut vincam miraculis Enoch et Heliam;
cum terris abstulero veritatis viam,
Rachel michi serviet, excecabo Liam.

Mea sunt cenobia, mei sunt claustrales,
mea sunt gimnasia, mee moniales,
sceptra regum mea sunt, mei cardinales,
per quos res ecclesie facio venales.

Ite, mei complices, ite, gentium di,
ite, despergimini per anfractus mundi;
caro factus sequar vos; sic enim spopondi."
At illi corripiunt fugam gemebundi). (#16)

This lurid fantasy nicely illustrates the satirical aims and techniques of Walter of Chatillon. He exposes the disordered world in general terms through the ironic and hyperbolic dialogue of fiends, while he also includes topical references (e.g., Becket's martyrdom, the papal schism). Two of his favorite themes, ecclesiastical corruption and royal animosity toward the Church and its prerogatives, are clearly revealed. He adroitly blends mythological figures (Furies, Cerberus and Pluto) with Scriptural (Beelzebub, Giezi, Rachel and Leah), ancient (Nero) with contemporary (Frederick). Allusions to the Bible (e.g., St. Paul as vas electionis in Acts. 9.15) and the classics, especially Vergil and Ovid, bespeak the erudition which characterizes Walter's poetry. His sharp and bitter diction unmask his seething indignation, his frustration. Moreover, the cadences of his powerful rhythms, heightened by constant end rhymes, evidence his extraordinary skills as a versifier. All these impressive features, and more, account for the honored place accorded to Walter of Chatillon's small collection in the history of Latin satire.

CHAPTER IV

NOTES

[1] Eighteen satirical poems were edited by Karl Strecker, Moralisch-Satirische Gedichte Walters von Chatillon (Heidelberg, 1929), from which all quotations in this study will be taken. Other poems by Walter or his "school" were edited by Strecker, Die Lieder Walters von Chatillon (Berlin, 1925) and André Wilmart, "Poèmes de Gautier de Chatillon dans un ms. de Charleville," Revue Bénédictine 49 (1937) 121-69 and 322-65. G. F. Whicher prints the texts and his own verse translations of five poems by Walter in The Goliard Poets (New York, 1965). Two useful studies are F. Chatillon, "Flagello sepe castigatus vitam terminavit: Contribution a L'Etude des mauvais traitements infligés a Gautier de Chatillon," Revue du Moyen Age Latin VII, no. 2 (1951) 151-62, and L. Eldredge, "Walter of Chatillon and the Decretum of Gratian: an Analysis of 'Propter Zion non tacebo'," Studies in Medieval Culture III (1970) 59-69.

[2] These images are employed in #1, 2 and 10.

[3] W. J. Millor, S. J. and C. N. L. Brooke, The Letters of John of Salisbury II (Oxford, 1979) 192-97 and 254-56.

[4] The literary character of Henry II's court is described by Peter Dronke, "Peter of Blois and Poetry at the Court of Henry II," Mediaeval Studies 38 (1976) 185-235.

[5] Marvin L. Colker, ed. Galteri de Castellione: Alexandreis (Padua, 1978).

[6] See the chapter on Walter of Chatillon in C. Witke, Latin Satire: the Structure of Persuasion (Leiden, 1970).

[7] Witke, 240.

[8] This same idea, which originates with Ovid, Ars Amatoria II.280, is in #6.7-8.

[9] Peter Dronke, "Profane Elements in Literature," in Renaissance and Renewal in the Twelfth Century, eds. R. L. Benson and G. Constable, with Carol D. Lanham (Cambridge, Ma., 1982) 582.

[10] Gilbert Highet, Juvenal the Satirist (N.Y., 1961 repr.) 40-41. See also Peter Green, Juvenal: The Sixteen Satires (Baltimore, Md., 1974) 35.

[11] The Biblical stories of Giezi and Simon Magus were popular among Medieval satirists and commentators as typical of the sale of sacred offices. See J. A. Yunck, The Lineage of Lady Meed (South Bend, Ind., 1963) 26.

[12] Two famous poems on Rome by Hildebert of Lavardin are printed as nos. 36 and 38 in Hildeberti Cenomanensis Episcopi carmina minora, ed. A. Brian Scott (Leipzig, 1969). See Yunck, 85-117.

[13] The Bakelfest is described by E. K. Chambers, The Mediaeval Stage I (Oxford, 1903) 274ff., and Karl Young, The Drama of the Medieval Church I (Oxford, 1933) 104-5.

[14] E. R. Curtius, European Literature and the Latin Middle Ages, trans. W. R. Trask (New York, 1963) 94-98.

[15] R. G. M. Nisbet, "Persius" in Satire, ed. J. P. Sullivan (Bloomington, Ind., 1968) 42; Janet Martin, "Uses of Tradition: Gellius, Petronius, and John of Salisbury," Viator 10 (1979) 68 points out that "one of the important uses of the classical tradition for John and his circle may have been the reinforcement of their sense of being a small group, an elite."

[16] Witke, 235-36 et passim.

[17] These puns are in #1.8.4-6; 8.12.1; 2.17.1-2; 15.19.4; 15.21.4. See also #5.22.1-4 where Walter puns extensively on the name Fulmarus, whose real identity is unknown.

[18] W. Wetherbee, The Cosmographia of Bernardus Silvestris (New York, 1973) 14. For a detailed explanation of the terms

involucrum and integumentum in allegory, see E. Jeauneau, "L'Usage de la notion d'integumentum a travers les gloses de Guillaume de Conches," Archives d'histoire doctrinale et litteráire du Moyen Age 32 (1957) 35-100. A standard book on the history of Medieval allegory is C. S. Lewis, The Allegory of Love (Oxford, 1936).

[19]Brian Tierney, The Crisis of Church and State 1050-1300 (Englewood Cliffs, N.J., 1964) 97-109 traces the role of Cardinal Rolandus, later Pope Alexander III, at the famous Diet of Besançon.

CHAPTER V
NIGEL OF CANTERBURY

**Terruit et rabidos parvula virga canes
- Nigel of Canterbury -**

The engaging humor and charm of Nigel of Canterbury's Speculum Stultorum (Mirror of Fools) led to its author's instant and sustained success. Contemporaries borrowed verses from this narrative of the amusing misadventures of Burnellus the ass, while the leading writers of subsequent generations, especially Nigel's countrymen, were indebted to him for examples, themes and characters in their own satires. John Gower appropriated numerous lines for his several books, and Geoffrey Chaucer cited "Daun Burnel the Asse" as the source for an exemplum in The Canterbury Tales. Most recently, Umberto Eco, in a clever allusion, transforms the ass into Brunellus, the abbot's favorite steed in The Name of the Rose.[1]

Nigel's works are endearing for their wit, venerable for their fervent moral posture, and admirable for their learning. Apart from his poetry and one prose treatise, however, little is known about the man.[2] Monastic authors, of course, commonly remain obscure figures, even when their writings achieve considerable fame. Nigel was a monk, and a priest, at Christchurch, Canterbury. Internal evidence in <u>Speculum Stultorum</u> reveals that he had some opportunities to travel, perhaps before entering the cloister, for his description of student life at Paris is undoubtedly derived from first-hand experience. His traditional surname, Longchamps, suggests that he was born in Normandy; another surname, Wireker, seems to be the invention of early literary historians. Nigel had to have arrived at Canterbury before 1170, for he claimed personal acquaintance with Archbishop Thomas Becket, who died on December 29 of that year.[3] In the opening line of the prologue to <u>Speculum Stultorum</u>, published in 1180, Nigel identified himself as <u>vetus</u> (old). Yet, he continued to write until at least 1194. He died at the end of the twelfth century or very early in the thirteenth.

Nigel's <u>Tractatus Contra Curiales et Officiales Clericos</u>, written toward the end of his life, was his major prose composition. The work is heavily dependent on the long, digressive <u>Policraticus</u>, published some thirty-five years earlier (1159) by another Canterbury man, John of Salisbury.[4] Though this is not the place to detail John's considerable influence on Nigel, I should point out that John, a secular clerk, enjoys a splendid reputation for erudition, loyalty to the Canterbury primacy, and a distinct penchant for satirical humor. These qualities are replicated in Nigel, who took up several of his older contemporary's themes and forms, including the elegiac metre of John's satirical <u>Entheticus</u> for his own verse satire. In addition to a small collection of shorter poems which have survived, Nigel also wrote an account of the passion of Saint Lawrence, a life of Paul the hermit, and a versified list of Canterbury archbishops. His seventeen hexameter poems on miracles of the Virgin Mary have been edited recently.[5]

Nigel's contribution to twelfth-century satire is Speculum Stultorum. This narrative of 3900 elegiac verses is, in my judgment, the finest example of the genre produced in the entire century. The extended, comical journey of the ass is a framework for parody, exempla, debate, proverbs, beast fable, and much more, all directed against contemporary abuses, and folly in general. The ostensible object of ridicule is Burnellus, an ass discontent with the length of his tail. He undertakes a trip in search of means to elongate his quite-normal tail, and, of course, a comic odyssey results. Burnellus symbolizes every man driven by vainglory to advance in worldly preferments beyond what his natural capabilities allow. Specifically, Nigel intended to signify ambitious monks who wished to become priors and abbots, as he explained in a letter to William of Longchamps, to whom he addressed several of his works.[6] Within the simple outline of this fable, however, Nigel has cleverly enveloped a host of social criticisms and witty insights into ludicrous human behavior. The wonderful medley which results is best studied, I think, by following the loose plot and pausing to analyze the manifold objects of satire in turn as they present themselves.

Speculum Stultorum opens with a verse prologue of eighty lines addressed to William. After expressing a commonplace affectation of rude matter and unpolished form, the poet immediately alerts his reader to the allegorical nature of the work. He alludes to Horace (Sermones 1. 1.24), suggesting that apparent trifles occasionally conceal serious lessons. He adds that short stories often encompass mighty mysteries, and a valuable item is sometimes hidden in rubbish. Nigel unfolds another satirical topos, the times gone mad, the world turned topsy-turvy.[7] However, he does not dwell at length on aberrations of nature, which other writers frequently did, but he moves swiftly to a familiar complaint within the genre: the arrogant rebellion of youth against authority. In the perennial conflict of generations, which manifested itself in the twelfth century opposition of the moderns (moderni) to the ancients (auctores), Nigel clearly favors the latter. With scornful irony, he describes the beardless boy (puer impubes) thought more eloquent than Cicero, more prudent than Cato; he mocks this mere lad who explains every mystery under heaven. Then our poet offers the rather severe reminder (echoing St. Matthew's gospel) that walls painted white outside may contain filth within, gold may overlay rotten wood. Nigel foreshadows the appearance of his central character and his return to this theme when he observes:

> Although an ass might hold the lion's realms and sceptre,
> And rule his subjects, he will always be an ass.
>
> (Regna licet teneat sceptrumque leonis asellus,
> Juraque det populis, semper asellus erit)
>
> (57-8)

The prologue draws to a close with the serious observation that an ass who plays lion might not only lose what he takes from him, but also might "unlearn" his own nature. The saner action would be not to seize another's possession than to lose one's own in disgrace. Thus, the stage is set for the entrance of Burnellus asellus, and the way is prepared for the satire of a society in which many appear to be what they are not. From the outset, Nigel has signaled a world awry, one in which unenlightened boys claim precedence over their elders, simple monks seek lofty advancements, asses rule in lions' places.

Nigel's actual narrative begins (line 81) with wondrous simplicity: once upon a time (<u>quondam</u>), a little ass with enormous ears (<u>auribus immensis</u>) decided that he should have a tail of equal length. Since he was unable to accomplish this himself, he consulted physicians, because he thought that they could perform by skill what Nature had not granted. No other details are given about this protagonist, not even his name, although the narrator assures us that the unamended tail was quite sufficient for use (<u>non quia longa satis non esset ad utilitatem</u>). Of course, the ass has been proverbially an obtuse beast from ancient times. Making one the central character in a story naturally invites the reader into a comic fable which he anticipates will be dominated by stubbornness, stupidity, and eventual disaster. Not only is the ass' objective rash and unnatural, but he compounds his foolishness by consulting doctors, men whose practices were also long-standing objects of satire.

The doctor in our story is appropriately named Galen (<u>Galienus</u>), after the famous physician-writer of Pergamum. In the Middle Ages, that name was synonymous with the medical profession. Nigel's use of it, however, may be more pointed. His educated audience would surely appreciate the contrast between patients, the wise Marcus Aurelius for the original Galen, and a doltish ass for his successor. Nevertheless, the later Galen delivers, albeit verbosely, sound advice, i.e., abandon the foolish design of lengthening the tail. His argument rests on several points: the tail is already adequate, and to tamper might diminish it; medical experiments are long and dangerous; only God is a true, healing physician (doctors with their herbs, drugs and ointments are merely His agents); the ass' immense ears easily compensate for the smaller tail, which, if longer, could be a source of greater ridicule and trouble; Nature's design cannot be contradicted by human arts. All this advice is rephrased and reiterated several times to mock the loquacity of the opinionated doctor. Of course, the main thrust of the passage is to deride in the figure of the ass those who foolishly seek preferments. Galen underscores this by direct address, repeatedly calling the ass absurd (inepte), immoderate (improbe), silly (stulte).

The talkative physician now proceeds to illustrate his moral with an exemplum of precipitous folly. In the first of three internal narratives in Speculum Stultorum, he recounts the story of two cows, Brunetta and Bicornis. He begins the detailed account by assuring the ass that he saw the cows, one black (nigra), the other reddish (flava), as a boy on his father's farm (puer aspexi). Once, a sudden frost hardened the rain-soaked pastures where the cattle grazed and fixed their tails in the frozen mud. After a night of exhausting but unsuccessful struggle to free themselves, Bicornis rashly cut off her own tail to escape the gripping ice. Brunetta waited for the thaw, which, in time, freed her. Her patience preserved her tail, the only weapon against the flies and wasps of summer, which so tormented the defenseless Bicornis that she died in misery.

This amusing fable could be conveyed in a passage of few lines. However, Nigel takes nearly four hundred (205-594), the length of an epyllion, to relate it. Clearly, this is for greater purpose than to mock the verbosity of the physician. The length allows the narrator to lend credibility to the story by a host of significant details (e.g., Bicornis' pathetic anxiety for her newborn calf) and enables him to display erudition (e.g., he cites legal precedents, the classics, proverbs). Moreover, the narrative is punctuated by clever speeches in which Bicornis rationalizes her actions, Brunetta refutes her arguments and commends the usefulness of a tail, and Bicornis pours out a remorseful lament. The entire story is enhanced by sound devices. For example the anaphora of <u>illa dies</u> (fourteen times in lines 405-41) parodies the dire prophecy of Sophonias (1.15) in the Old Testament, while alliteration of the letter "m" echoes the lowing of the distraught cow in her final agony:

> Death is sweet to the wretched, a gentle solace to me,
> Nothing can be more gentle to the wretched than death.
>
> (Dulce mori miseris, mors est mihi mite levamen,
> Morte nihil miseris mitius esse potest) (571-2)

In fact, this effect is sustained by the repetition of <u>mors</u> in eight consecutive lines (569-76).

The obvious lesson of the fable is patience, a virtue explicitly attributed to Brunetta (<u>minus haec praeceps prudensque magis patienter</u>). The warning is clear against the opposite extreme, rashness, which destroys Bicornis, whose actions are sometimes modified by <u>praeceps</u>, a word meaning "headlong" or "hasty" (e.g., lines 464, 473, 550, 557). One couplet of her closing address expresses this moral:

I have lived an example to many, and an example
For all to come I die, one having no moderation.

(Exemplum multis vixi moriorque futuris
Omnibus exemplum, non habitura modum) (577-8)

For all the good sense of this lesson alone, however, Bicornis is not quite finished. She adds three further cautions, all introduced by the word discite (learn): vainglory is neighbor to ruin; transitory pleasure is nothing; rashness causes destruction. These admonitions were surely directed at those monks of Canterbury and elsewhere who sought the glory of preferments in the cloister or worldly pleasures without; they warn against the rashness which might imperil the monk's spiritual life and ultimate salvation. This explains the thematic function of illa dies and mors discussed above, and the repetition of vae vae (woe woe) in Bicornis' lament (461-68).

At the conclusion of his exemplum, Galen attempts once more to dissuade the ass, now called Burnellus (line 595) for the first time. He says quite plainly, "you are a fool; go home," (stultus es; ito domum). However, the crafty physician adds immediately that a tail could be lengthened, at great expense, of course! In short, the ass is dispatched to Salerno to fill an impossible prescription. Among its carefully-measured ingredients are fat from marble, hawks' milk, a mite's liver, and snow which has fallen on Saint John's day (in June!). The absurdity of this extensive recipe satirizes medical quackery, and symbolizes the ridiculous aims of those malcontents who seek happiness in unworthy pursuits. Charlatans and worldly monks are the objects of playful scorn as

Galen reiterates thrice that he hopes his and Burnellus' efforts (<u>cura laborque</u>) will not be wasted. He imparts a farewell blessing upon his patient. It concludes with these words:

> May hail, snow, rain accompany you everywhere,
> And may white frost cover you with ice at night.
> May hateful hounds be often at your back!
> To which the little ass, bestowing kisses, said Amen!
>
> (Grando, nives, pluviae tecum comitentur ubique,
> Protegat et noctu cana pruina gelu!
> Saepius exosus veniat post terga molossus!
> Oscula dando tamen dixit asellus, Amen!)
>
> (679-82)

Burnellus' journey to Salerno provides the framework for satire of two more disreputable classes, merchants and peasants. After an exhaustive search throughout the city for goods that did not exist anywhere in the world, the ass was spied by a merchant named Truffator (Swindler), who had come there from his home, London, to find medicines to heal the snub-nose of his master, the bishop. The merchant's typical deceptions include flattery, empathy and the assurance that from a fellow-stranger he will only recover costs, no profit! Of course, Burnellus is duped, and buys ten large jars filled with trifles (<u>nugis</u>). Nigel's satire of a universal rogue, the crafty merchant, has special import for his countrymen since Truffator, and his sister, Gula (Gluttony), are English. Another example of topicality in this passage may be the reference to the bishop with the short nose. Gilbert Foliot of London had been a leading adversary of Becket, and was considered no friend of Canterbury, as John of Salisbury's letters clearly prove.[8]

As part of his fawning, the London merchant asks Burnellus his worthy name (<u>nomen dignum</u>). The ass responds and claims that his noble office is to serve princes and kings. This boast prompts him to a bitter tirade against the plague (<u>pestis</u>), that deadly evil (<u>exitiale malum</u>), the harsh peasant (<u>rusticus immitis</u>) with his damned dogs, sharp goads and knotted whips. Many satirical forms, including the popular fabliaux, ridiculed the boorish behavior of rustics, whose ignominious penalties were viewed as fitting consequences of malice or stupidity. Nigel's contribution to this commonplace takes the form of a brief contrast between the manners of nobles and the <u>furcifer</u> (fork-bearing) <u>rusticus</u>, followed by a curse on the latter:

> May the mange assail him, fever burn him up,
> So that he cannot ride a horse, nor walk on foot.
> May evil lumps settle in his throat, torment his head,
> And may his bowels flow night and day.
> May his stern lord advance to long life,
> And may he and his wife always quarrel.
> From the sole of his foot right up to his face
> May sores inflame, swarming with worms and decay.
> I commend him to Satan, from whose shit
> He is said to be sprung, which he proves enough.
> If I could delete him from the face of the earth,
> There would be no place for him in city or world.

(Impetat hunc scabies, hunc cotidiana perurat,
Ne possit vel eques ipse vel ire pedes.
Faucibus insideat mala gutta caputque fatiget,
Defluat et venter nocte dieque suus.
Durus ei dominus longum succedat in aevum,
Rixentur semper uxor et ipse simul.
Hunc pedis a planta summotenus ore perurant
Ulcera, quae scateant vermibus atque lue.
Hunc ego commendo Sathanae, de stercore cujus
Dicitur esse satus, quod probat ipse satis.
Hunc ego si possem totum delere per orbem,
Nullus ei fieret urbe vel orbe locus.) (811-22)

This brief imprecation, a parody of the formal ecclesiastical anathema, is doubly funny. Placed in the mouth of an ass, it is a ridiculous imitation of a serious practice, and the blights he invokes upon his adversary are perversely comical in themselves. Nigel creates here an especially delightful incongruity.

The satire thus far has comically exposed the vices of the unstable monk (in the figure of the ass), the physician, merchant and peasant. Now, as Burnellus advances homeward, he confronts his most dangerous assailant, a Cistercian monk. This simple encounter, like the narrative of the cows, is elaborated in detail, with dialogue and speeches, so that its length approaches four hundred lines (827-1220). A proverbial couplet foreshadows the imminent disaster:

> In happy circumstances, how near is ruin
> And a quick fall, no one can see!

(Casibus in laetis quam sit vicina ruina
Et lapsus facilis nemo videre potest!) (827-8)

The unwary Burnellus, following a worn path through fields near Lyon, is attacked by huge dogs. The hounds have been unleashed by Brother Fromund, actually a laybrother (conversus) assigned farm chores on monastery lands. Burnellus tries to flee, the vases he carries are shattered, their precious contents are lost, and, worst of all, half the ass' tail is bitten off. The malicious monk, who approaches laughing (Extendensque manum, dicto benedicite, ha! ha!) is soon terrified himself, for Burnellus claims repeatedly to be a servant of the Pope. This outrage will cost the order dearly, he threatens. Brother Fromund, under the guise of offering reparation, invites Burnellus to a country retreat, "another Paradise" (alter Paradisus), intending there to kill him. Along the way, however, the ass pushes the monk off a cliff into the Rhone, where he drowns. This portion of the poem concludes with a victory paean by Burnellus, and his reflections on his past folly. Fearing ridicule at home for his failed mission, he resolves to get an education and return in triumph.

Once again, Nigel has offered his reader a brilliant satiric medley. Two objects of ridicule especially stand out in this encounter between Burnellus and Fromund: the Cistercian order, and vainglory. The white monks were favorite targets of Anglo-Latin satirists, as I have noted earlier. Nigel returns to them later in his general review of orders, but here he directs his clever mockery toward a concrete example, Brother Fromund. First, the setting itself, a large farm estate, testifies to the wealth and expansion of the order. Then, Fromund is shown to be malicious and inhospitable in attacking a harmless wayfarer crossing his fields. With the expression "in the manner of his brothers" (fratrum de more suorum), Nigel goes on to confirm the monk's gluttony and lax spirituality as he describes his approach:

> Yet not hurrying, except when impelled to the cook's pot,
> As he is wont, his belly pointing the way to table.
> But walking with spondaic foot, an ass' pace,
> As he is wont to come to prayers at night.
>
> (Non tamen accelerans, nisi cum pulsatur ad ollam,
> Ut solet, ad mensam ventre docente viam;
> Sed pede spondaico gressu gradiens asinino,
> Ut solet ad laudes nocte venire, venit.) (881-4)

Later, when Burnellus announces the Pope's terms of retribution for Fromund's crime, Nigel alludes to the order's exemption from tithes (decimas), its restriction on wearing breeches (braccae), its frequent neglect of the vow of stability (claustra nec exibunt), its reputed fondness for wine (vina) and cooked foods (nisi cruda legumina), all sources of ridicule in twelfth-century satires on Cistercian customs. Fromund is even made to confess fear of his own religious brothers, for their fury knows no bounds. As Walter Map's prose would do, though much more fiercely, Nigel's verses single out the white monks for a special measure of satirical criticism.

As a transition to his theme of vainglory, Nigel inserts a song of victory (1075-1100) in which Burnellus invites the asses of the world to celebrate his triumph over Fromund. It begins:

> Comrades, let us sing! Asses, let us feast!
> Let our instruments sound with words and wishes.
> Let asses exult, let joyous asses play,
> With festive praise let drums, rattles, dances sound.
>
> (Cantemus, socii! festum celebremus, aselli!
> Vocibus et votis organa nostra sonent.
> Exultent asini, laeti modulentur aselli,
> Laude sonent celebri tympana, sistra, chori!)
>
> (1075-8)

The passage is superbly ironic -- asses triumphant -- and a wonderful parody of the victory paeans which occur so frequently in heroic narratives. In these delightful lines, and the description of Fromund's epitaph which follows, our poet repeats the proper name eight times, often coupling it with the words <u>frater</u>, <u>fraus</u>, and <u>fallere</u> (brother, fraud, to deceive). Such alliteration contributes to the mock epic, and may point to some topical significance in the name itself. Coincidentally, <u>Garin le Loherain</u>, a contemporary <u>chanson de geste</u>, has a villain named "Fromont."[9] The closing words of Fromund's epitaph invite his hostile brothers (<u>fratres iniqui</u>) to remember his deadly fall and to keep his example in mind.

As Burnellus resumes his homeward journey, he becomes reflective, then melancholy, as he contemplates his abiding foolishness in advancing age. Again the ridiculous exaggerations of the ass are underscored by repetitions and alliterations. For example, in lines 1114-1123 of Burnellus' meditation, the words <u>saepe</u>, <u>semper</u> and <u>stultus</u> (often, always, foolish) occur ten times;

his conventional discourse on the burdens of old age (1131-42) employs sensus and senex (understanding, old) ten times. In short, the excessive repetition confirms Burnellus' observation: he has always been stupid, and age has not cured him. Thus, scornful laughter awaits him at home. Burnellus resolves not to return there until his wits have been sharpened by scholastic discipline (sensus hebes studiis exacuendus erit). He will study the Arts at Paris for ten years, Law at Bologna, and finally, the queen of sciences, Theology. He envisions a glorious homecoming then, when his reputation will precede him, and titles of honor will announce his arrival. The people will rush forward to declare, "Behold, the master is here!" (Ecce, Magister adest). The distinction of his new title will compensate for his lost tail, his overlong ears. "The final glory will cover all faults" (Gloria finalis crimina cuncta teget).

The clear thrust of Nigel's satire is mockery of the shallow aspirations of those who seek insubstantial glory in a title, a name. In this aim, Nigel joins other satirists of the period, notably John of Salisbury, whose Entheticus (esp. lines 39-122) brilliantly exposes the vainglory of students and masters who would rather seem learned than be so. Burnellus' intention is to shield himself from derision with an exalted title, though he entirely lacks the ability to earn it. In fact, his nature opposes learning and makes him ever-dull. So, implies the poet, are many (monks) who rashly pursue academic attainments for which they are unsuited by nature and by temperament. Their end can only be the scornful laughter which greets an aged ass in a master's gown.

On his way to Paris, Burnellus meets Arnold, a Sicilian with the same destination. They become traveling companions, and in their self-introductions, Burnellus rehearses briefly what has happened to him thus far, while Arnold's response is the second internal narrative of the poem, an <u>exemplum</u> of wrath and revenge. He tells the story of Gundulf, the son of a priest in Apulia. The boy often carried a stick with which he chased away the chickens from his father's grain store. Once, his zeal for this task exceeded proper bounds, and in a fit of anger the lad broke the shin-bone of a cockerel with a sharp blow. In time, the leg healed, but never the heart. The cock longed for revenge, and seized the chance which presented itself. On the day appointed for Gundulf's own ordination, his earnest desire, the cock refused to crow. The sleeping household slumbered on past the hour of the ceremony, and Gundulf missed the opportunity to succeed his father in the holy office.

Of course, Nigel amplifies this long narrative (1251-1502) with his customary wealth of detail. He has Arnold lend credence to the story by claiming to have seen Gundulf with his own eyes (<u>quem vidimus ipsi</u>). He carefully describes the boy's cruel offense, the cock's abiding resentment, and the dire consequences. He interweaves appropriate allusions, proverbs, an extended dialogue between the vengeful cock and Coppa, his reproachful hen, and a nightmare which foreshadows Gundulf's approaching calamity. The lordly cock and his mistress, as well as the prophetic dream, were adopted by Chaucer for his "Nun's Priest's Tale." In fact, the sly fox in that tale refers explicitly to Nigel's anecdote:

> I have wel rad in "Daun Burnel the Asse,"
> Among his vers, how that ther was a cok,
> For that a preestes sone yaf hym a knok

> Upon his leg whil he was yong and nyce,
> He made hym for to lese his benefice.)
>
> (3312-16)

The satirical point of the exemplum is aimed at the vice of wrath, which includes revenge. As Arnold establishes the context of his illustrative story, he often uses the terms ultio (revenge), ira (anger) and vindicta (vengeance). He dwells on the psychology of recrimination, underscored by the repeated phrase mens laesa (the offended mind), concluding:

> Neither does a duck long to see a pool, nor wolf a fleeing lamb
> Nor pack of hounds the hare, nor snared beast her escape,
> Nor a fish water, nor the hawk the lark,
> More than the offended mind to see swift vengeance.
>
> (Non mergus stagnum, fugientem non lupus agnum,
> Turba canum leporem, vel fera capta fugam;
> Nec plus piscis aquam, nec avet plus nisus alaudam,
> Quam mens vindictam laesa videre citam.) (1305-8)

Clearly, Nigel satirizes those monks who, like the cock, harbor resentments and seek opportunities for revenge. Gundulf represents those who exercise authority with cruel rigor, angry themselves and provoking that emotion in their brothers. These are surely the primary objects of satire, though the reader is often treated to rapid gibes at others, as, for example, simony (the ordaining bishop acceded to the "prayers and merits of Saint Ruffinus," the mock-patron of bribes) and revelry (the household oversleeps because Bacchus and the guests at the pre-ordination feast indulge too much in food and drink). At story's end, Arnold draws the moral which fathers often impart to their sons: govern your behavior everywhere, lest later you regret it.

The next section (1503-1912) of Speculum Stultorum describes Burnellus' sojourn at Paris. The main satirical object here, as Nigel himself explained in his epistle to William, is the monk who insists on undertaking higher studies in order to seem learned, when in fact he lacks the proper motivation and ability for these pursuits. Such pretense (simulatio is Nigel's word) will inevitably be discovered, as when the ass leaves Paris after seven years of study unable to recall even the name of the city. Of course, Nigel cleverly intersperses numerous other witty observations and digressions into the narrative, including a sardonic description of English scholars, wry commentaries on student poverty and on dream interpretation, a mockery of the pretensions of abbots, and a serious outline of a bishop's proper virtues. Here is the first portion of Burnellus' stay at the famous schools of Paris:

> When, walking together, they had recounted many such stories,
> They enter Paris and seek an inn.
> Rest renews their weary bodies, and for the harm of a
> Meagre diet, a full table and many cups compensate.
> Bones, skin, tendons, which fatigue or the long journey
> Had enfeebled, baths, care and rest revive.
> Burnellus lets blood and trims his hair,
> And clothes himself with his best tunic.
> Combed and washed, at last having proceeded into the city,

He enters a church and offers vows and prayers.
From there, approaching the schools, he weighs whether
This one or that one is more advantageous to himself.
And since he observed that the English were subtle,
For many reasons he associated himself with them.
Excellent in character, pleasing in speech and looks,
They are rich in talent and esteemed for prudence.
They shower gifts upon people, and they loathe the greedy;
They multiply dishes of food and drink without restraint.
"Wassail," "Drinkheyl" and a female friend:
These three are the vices which attend them.
With these three excepted, there is nothing to reproach;
If you remove these three, all else is pleasing.
Yet, these are not so reprehensible that for them
There is not able to be a time and place.
For two especially drive away sorrows,
And they are wont to introduce the ways of gladness.
The third restrains the harm of liquorous passion
With which Gaul is said to be filled.
Hence he longed to be a wise companion to the English,
That he might be able to enjoy their mode of life.
There is even among these a certain reason (as common rumor
Imagines) why he wishes more to be joined to them;
If character is formed from living together,
Why would nothing increase for him if he were their comrade?
If Nature provides anything for them beyond their share,
Why would he carry hence nothing good before or behind?
Hastening, therefore, he adhered zealously to study

That he might learn to speak wittily and correctly.
But since his understanding is dull, his head very hard,
  He retains not the master's teachings; his efforts are wasted.
Now Burnellus has passed through many seasons,
  And his seventh year was nearly finished,
But nothing at all, whatever his master or associate
  Were teaching, could he learn except "Hee, Haw."
What Nature gave, what he brought there with him,
  This he has; this no one could take from him.
The solicitude of his masters, striving much and long,
  At last failed, overcome by heavy toil.
The rod lands often on his back, the stick in his side,
  And his hands endure the whip.
Always he repeats "Hee, Haw;" there is nothing which he
  Can say, moved by any lash, except "Hee, Haw."
This one plucks his ear, that one strikes his curved nose,
  This one knocks out his teeth, that one pierces his hide.
One cuts, one burns, here he is loosed, there bound,
  This man threatens, that one pleads.
Thus, in him Art and Nature contend in turn,
  Art asks, Nature orders, one goes, the other stays.
Those whose beginnings are shown to have been defective
  Are scarcely, or never, able to recover.
From boyhood Burnellus learned "Hee, Haw;" Nothing
  Beyond what Nature gives can he retain.
Nature saves what was inborn; what is of Art
Disappears as dust is wont to vanish in the wind.
He wasted his money; his every effort and everything
  Which he expended were lost equally.

Also the hope of extending his tail perished,
And he perceived that the English charms would be false.

(Talia cum pariter gradientes plura referrent,
  Parisius subeunt hospitiumque petunt.
Corpora fessa quies recreat, tenuisque diaetae
  Damna recompensat mensa calixque frequens.
Ossa, cutem, nervos, quae vel labor aut via longa
  Quassarat, refovent balnea, cura, quies;
Burnellusque sibi minuit crinesque totondit,
  Induit et tunica se meliore sua.
Pexus et ablutus tandem progressus in urbem
  Intrat in ecclesiam, vota precesque facit.
Inde scholas adiens secum deliberat utrum
  Expediat potius ista vel illa sibi.
Et quia subtiles sensu considerat Anglos,
  Pluribus ex causis se sociavit eis.
Moribus egregii, verbo vultuque venusti,
  Ingenio pollent consilioque vigent.
Dona pluunt populis et detestantur avaros,
  Fercula multiplicant et sine lege bibunt.
Washeyl et drinkheyl necnon persona secunda,
  Haec tria sunt vitia quae comitantur eis;
His tribus exceptis nihil est quod in his reprehendas;
  Haec tria si tollas, cetera cuncta placent.
Nec tamen haec ita sunt semper reprobanda, quod illis
  Esse locus nequeat tempore sive loco.
Nam duo praecipue sunt exclusiva dolorum,
  Laetitiaeque vias insinuare solent;
Tertia res cohibet, quo dicitur esse referta

Gallia fermentum ne nocuisse queat.
Hinc comes Angligenis prudens desiderat esse,
  Possit ut illorum conditione frui.
Est in eis etiam quiddam (ceu publica fama
  Somniat) adjungi cur magis optet eis,
Si de convictu mores formantur eidem,
  Cur nihil accrescat si comes esse queat?
Si quid eis praeter sortem natura ministrat,
  Ante retrove bonum cur nihil inde ferat?
Accelerans igitur studio studiosus adhaesit,
  Ut discat lepide grammaticeque loqui.
Sed quia sensus hebes, cervix praedura, magistri
  Dogmata non recipit, cura laborque perit.
Jam pertransierat Burnellus tempora multa,
  Et prope completus septimus annus erat,
Cum nihil ex toto, quodcunque docente magistro
  Aut socio, potuit discere praeter hy ha.
Quod natura dedit, quod secum detulit illuc,
  Hoc habet, hoc illi nemo tulisse potest.
Cura magistrorum multumque diuque laborans
  Demum defecit, victa labore gravi.
Dorso se baculus, lateri se virga frequenter
  Applicat, et ferulam sustinuere manus.
Semper hy ha repetit, nihil est quod dicere possit
  Affectus quovis verbere praeter hy ha.
Vellicat hic aurem, nasum quatit ille recurvum,
  Excutit hic dentes, perforat ille cutem.
Hic secat, hic urit, hinc solvitur, inde ligatur
  Intonat iste minas, porrigit ille preces.
Sic in eo certant ars et natura vicissim,

> Ars rogat, illa jubet, haec abit, illa manet.
> Quorum principia constant vitiosa fuisse,
> Aut vix aut nunquam convaluisse valent.
> A puero didicit Burnellus hy ha, nihil ultra
> Quam quod natura dat retinere potest.
> Quod fuit innatum servat natura, quod artis
> Sic abit, ut vento pulvis abire solet.
> Perdidit expensas, periit labor omnis et omne
> Quod fuit impensum conditione pari.
> Spes quoque deperiit caudae superinstituendae,
> Sensit et Anglorum carmina falsa fore)
>
> (1503-70)

Burnellus' narrative continues in this vein, as the ass becomes more and more disillusioned by the Paris schools, and discouraged at his own lack of progress. In fact, he has "unlearned" (dedidicisse) what he knew before. His reflections begin to resemble the lamentations of Job, only to be reversed suddenly by a new infusion of naive optimism. Who knows what fate holds in store? Perhaps the Fates will place a mitre on his head one day! He may become a bishop, but never an abbot! These suggestions lead directly to a satire on the pretensions of abbots, who did not enjoy the full authority and privileges of bishops. Even their mitres were shorter. Thus, Burnellus crudely likens bishops to stallions, but abbots to mules. Of course, the entire passage is another example of topicality in Nigel's medley.

The positive, salutary effect of satire is nicely illustrated in the brief section (1733-78) which concludes Burnellus' contrast of abbots and bishops. Beginning with the conventional image of the open book (Pontificis vita liber est), the poet rehearses all the noble qualities and requisite virtues of a true bishop, e.g., let him be wise, filled with the Spirit of God, a staff to the lame, a light to the blind, and so on. The idealized portrait, resting on abundant Scriptural allusions, reminds one of Chaucer's "povre Persoun," similarly distinguished among the reprobates and rascals of the world. The serious soon gives way again to the foolish, however, as Burnellus lapses into silly vainglory which so markedly contrasts the humility of the devout bishop just upheld to view. Nigel excludes the unworthy pursuits of fame (fama) and praise (laus) from the bishop's life, only to have stupid Burnellus meditate on exactly that vision of himself:

> And so, when I shall be promoted to bishop in my city,
>   No one in the whole world will be my equal.
> The people will come forth from the city to meet me,
>   And with heads bowed will say, "Hail, Bishop!"
> Then, I ask, what will my mother be able to say
>   When she sees me bless clergy and people?
> Made glad, she will bless the day, the season, the hour
>   In which, so blessed, she bore me as her son.
> And in how great a glory will my father rejoice
>   When they call him "lord" and "father of the bishop"

> (Ergo cum fuero praesul promotus in urbe,
>   In toto mundo par mihi nullus erit.
> Obvius exibit populus mihi totus ab urbe,
>   Dicet et obstipo vertice, "Praesul, ave!"
> Quid mea tunc mater, cum me benedicere clerum
>   Viderit et populum, dicere, quaeso, potest?

> Exhilarata diem tempus benedicet et horam,
> Qua peperit natum me benedicta suum;
> Et pater ille meus quanto gaudebit honore,
> Cum dominum dicent pontificisque patrem?)
>
> (1779-88)

Burnellus' fantasy leads directly to an <u>exemplum</u> (1804-1912) on ingratitude. The ass notes that the prefect (<u>praepositus</u>) of his city is likely to block his advancement, because Burnellus once rescued the man, a thief, from prison and saved him from execution. He recalls a popular proverb which declares that those whom one saves from deserved punishment become most dangerous enemies. There is a comic thrust to the story in the fawning gratitude expressed by the thief and his two companions as the ass secures their liberty and even transports them all to safety on his back. Alliterative effusion heightens this comedy, as the prisoners declare again and again "we are yours" (<u>sumus ecce tui</u>), and use expressions containing <u>tu</u>, <u>tuus</u>, <u>tibi</u> to ingratiate themselves. Of course, once free, the robbers never want to see again the one who might incriminate them. As he closes this illustration of the vice of ingratitude, Burnellus links it to low-born nature (<u>naturae servilis conditionis</u>) in yet another barb at the peasant class, while he reminds the nobility of their obligation:

> For this is wont to be a sign of noble blood,
> To wish to pay back a worthy recompense for favors.
>
> (Nam solet hoc proprium generosi sanguinis esse,
> Condignam meritis reddere velle vicem) (1905-6)

Nigel returns to the main satiric object of his protagonist's sojourn at Paris when he shows Burnellus unable to remember even the name of the city as soon as he departs. Such is his profit for seven years in the schools that he wonders if the city at his back is Rome! Only the salutation of a peasant reminds him of the name, Paris, which the ass resolves to repeat over and over for fifteen days lest he forget it again. Unfortunately, at the inn where Burnellus spends his twelfth night, a wayfarer recites many <u>Pater nosters</u> aloud. This boggles the ass' mind entirely, for the first syllable, "Pa," is the same as in his word. He forgets "Paris" again. Such incredible obtuseness, reminiscent of Rabelais' Gargantua, drives home the point that those unfit for higher studies will waste time and money in their pursuit, even at the famous schools of Paris. The passage as a whole (1913-2050) also mocks the institutions themselves, and contains a clever parody of formal logic and academic disputation as Burnellus reasons that to know something is better than nothing, neither is the whole lost as long as part remains. Thus, to recall only "Pa" is something, and for Burnellus, "not a little." Besides, too much study oppresses the brain. Better to <u>seem</u> knowledgeable in a few areas than to burden oneself with too much study. These conclusions lead the ass to reflect on the inability of knowledge to dispel the fear of death, and he rapidly turns his thoughts toward salvation. His decision to enter religious life marks a transition to a new satirical object, the orders.

The review of religious orders is a form of invective created by Anglo-Latin satirists of the twelfth century.[10] Besides our Nigel, three writers often cited as inventors and contributors to it are John of Salisbury, Walter Map and Gerald of Wales, all three secular clerks. The latter two, who reserved a particularly venomous enmity for Cistercians, wrote after Nigel, and both died in the first quarter of the thirteenth century. All three reviewed the orders in prose. Speculum Stultorum, then, is the only major poem on the religious orders by a monk. Its internal view, however, does not differ markedly from the sly insinuations and overt accusations of the "outside" observers. John of Salisbury, whose Policraticus (1159) antedates our poem by a quarter century, acknowledged the devout purposes and good works of several orders before he assailed laxity or vice among their members. He concluded (7.23) that members who equal the greatest saints might be discovered in each of the orders (in quavis earum forte reperientur qui possint sanctis superioribus adaequari). Nigel's practice in Speculum Stultorum is similar, though each order he cites is clearly marked for ridicule.

As Burnellus reflects on his new vocation, he considers eleven separate orders. Nigel's pattern is to have the ass introduce the order by name or by its particular habit, devotion, or the like. This is usually done in a single couplet, followed immediately by ironic "praise," innuendo and mockery. Thus, as one meets the Knights Templar with red crosses, Hospitallers with white crosses, Cluniacs in black, Austin Canons in white with black capes, he is reminded of Chaucer's careful distinctions in the garb of his Canterbury pilgrims. The satire moves from trivial prohibitions (e.g., the Templars may not gallop on horseback!) to circumvention of rules (Praemonstratensians abstain from all meat, but they eat the fat) to outright vices of avarice, gluttony and lust. Often Burnellus' naive compliments and innocent wonderment contain the richest humor, as when he marvels that the Grandmontines possess absolutely nothing, and yet they lack nothing, or the Cistercians, content with little (paucis contenti) do not cease to seek more.

Nigel's treatment of the religious orders is uneven, ranging from seven lines at the least (Hospitallers) to seventy-one (Cistercians). The entire section runs to over four hundred lines (2050-2454), including a passage in which Burnellus creates a new order by combining the "best" features of the existing ones. Though his criticisms of the Cistercians are the most extensive, and include their greedy acquisition of lands and flocks, along with strong hints of immorality and treachery, the most severe censures are directed at the Secular Canons. The fifty-five verses aimed at them are not funny, nor tempered by Nigel's gentle irony. They are entirely hostile in sentiment. He accuses the Secular Canons of unrestrained license, worldliness, hypocrisy: they subvert the foundation of the Faith; because of them, the strength of bishops wavers and kings contemplate iniquity. He even strings together lists of nasty epithets to call them, more a device of Bernard of Morval's complaints than Nigel's Horatian manner. Perhaps influenced by John of Salisbury's development of an organic theory of the state (Policraticus 5.6-11), Nigel compares the Secular Canons to the left sides of kings, to wandering feet, lying tongues, grasping hands, deceitful hearts.[11] He describes their lives as toilsome, their ways as slippery; their glory is dung, their end doubtful, their reward certain sorrow.

The writers who assailed the religious orders drew upon a common store of material, from petty infractions to serious crime, from ribald jokes to scandalous immorality. Speculum Stultorum, however, contains one unique passage (2371-2400) in twelfth-century Anglo-Latin satire, that on the nuns (ordo velatarum mulierum, quas etiam nonnas dicimus). This also turns bitter. After a few complimentary phrases on the holy (<u>sacras</u>) virgins and widows who keep the canonical hours both night and day, Burnellus suddenly likens their chant to siren songs. They are called serpents in body, sirens in voice, dragons at heart, Susannas outwardly, but Paris (i.e., seducers) within. Yet, they cover all faults with their tears, which flow without restraint (<u>quae sine lege fluunt</u>). However, their dazzling white limbs (<u>candida membra</u>) beneath their black tunics, the absence of girdles and leggings, hint at sexual promiscuity, which Burnellus makes plain by charging that some are barren, others are bearing (<u>parientes</u>)! In one bold obscenity, he declares:

> She who is granted the honor of a pastor's rod,
> That one indeed bears better and more fertilely.
>
> (Quae pastoralis baculi donatur honore,
> Illa quidem melius fertiliusque parit)
>
> (2397-8)

The review of orders is another example of Nigel's skillful satire, a true blend of the ironic, humorous, and obscene, with abrupt alternations of tone when the author shifts from levity to trenchant invective. There are numerous topical allusions and historical references as well, such as the Hospitallers' service in the Holy Land (<u>ad Libanum</u>), the schism which divided the Grandmontines for many years, and the "new" English order, the Gilbertines of Sempringham (<u>Simplingham</u>). Burnellus even fears that to join the Knights Templar might lead to the Saladin making laces from his skin! Thus, popular rumor and the author's own insights are complemented by important historical facts.

Burnellus closes his review by deciding to establish his own community, adopting one rule from each order. His new constitution is ridiculous, of course, but it does give the reader a clear sense of the outstanding satirical target in individual orders. The singular virtue which Burnellus selects from each is, naturally, the least strenuous or most suggestive. A few are distortions of innocent allowances in a given rule. The ass establishes the laws of his order as follows: to spare his monks walking, from the Templars he accepts horses; from Hospitallers, lying (<u>mentiri</u>) anywhere; from Cluniacs, permission to eat fat; to wear no breeches at night, from the Cistercians; talkativeness from Grandmontines; to attend but one mass a month from the solitary Carthusians; meat from Austin Canons and soft garments from Praemonstratensians; a female companion (<u>persona secunda</u>) from the Secular Canons; to wear no girdle from the nuns. Though he is uncertain what to adopt from the Gilbertines, since they are so recent a foundation of men and women together, he decides upon the rule that no sister may remain with a brother, except secretly (<u>nisi clam nulloque sciente</u>)! Burnellus will name the new order after himself, that his name might live forever.   He sets out for Rome to secure the Pope's approbation.

Nigel turned his attention next (2465-2922) to the second form of invective created by twelfth-century Anglo-Latin writers.[12] This <u>satira communis</u>, or "general satire," surveyed the classes of society, much as the review of orders had done for those in religious life. The story accomodates this shift by having Burnellus meet Doctor Galen once again, and rehearse briefly the hardships he has experienced since leaving home. The ass laments the sorry state of morality in the world (<u>tot et tanta miseri sunt scandala mundi, tot</u>

regum scelera pontificumque mala) in lines reminiscent of the unrelieved negativism of Bernard of Morval. In fact, such mournful outpouring seems to be the conventional prelude to satira communis. The chief cause (praemaxima causa) of Burnellus' unceasing tears is the Roman Curia, whose reputed corruption and venality surely invited more satirical assaults than any other medieval institution. To underscore the moral depravation of the curia at Rome, Burnellus reflects on its former glory in a series of some twenty laudatory epithets (e.g., solis radius; malleus erroris; justitiae gladius; morum gloria), several of which are drawn from Scripture. These conclude with the observation that the head (caput) of the world has become the tail (cauda). The remainder of the passage plays upon the familiar motifs of greed (semper avara sitit) and bribery (bursa referta reos solvit), returning several times to the popular image of Rome as the world's head. As the entire body suffers when the head aches, so the entire world feels the ill effects of Rome's avarice.[13] Given his education, Nigel surely realized that his theme was well-worn, for he employed a topos (the long life of Nestor would not suffice to tell all he could) to abandon it. His last words on the Roman Curia echo the prophet Isaiah (1.6):

> From the top of the head even to the sole of the foot,
> I think that nothing healthy remains in it.
>
> (A summo capitis in ea pedis usque deorsum
> Ad plantam sanum nil superesse reor.) (2557-8)

The poet sustains the tone of bitter invective as Burnellus' discourse turns next to kings. The point of the review (regum mores vitamque revolvam) is predictable: kings are fickle, too harsh, tyrannical, not rulers, but robbers (non rectores sed raptores). Though the charges leveled at kings are sweeping, there is one topical reference (2663-70) to England's forest laws, an object of satire also in John of Salisbury's Entheticus.[14] Most of the extensive passage, however, is a digression on the pervasive evil of gifts, i.e., bribes. The word munera introduces twenty-eight elegiac couplets in series, and the word actually occurs thirty-six times between lines 2593-2649. Nigel's sustained anaphora is one of the longer examples in Latin poetry, though the device was a favorite among medieval versifiers, especially satirists who generalized endlessly on the influence of gifts (munera), money (pecunia) and coin (nummus).[15] Nigel's contribution to this commonplace is a rehearsal of the inexhaustible powers of bribes: to bring peace and to declare war, to establish laws and to destroy them, to make the tongues of fools eloquent, and so on. "Love conquers all," he echoes (from Vergil), "but bribes conquer even love. If one doubts this, let him weigh both!" As the long series nears completion, the poet's formula becomes munera si cessant (if bribes should cease) to introduce the good effects which would result, e.g., God might return to Cluniac houses; Judas and Simon Magus would be expelled by the clergy; crying, grief and sorrow would be no more. These sentiments of Nigel's satira communis are so sharply expressed, so indisputable as to cause the reader to forget that they are being exclaimed in the raucous braying of Burnellus the ass.

The complaints against bishops occupy a longer passage (2665-2814), for they are more guilty, Burnellus affirms, than kings. The charges are drawn from the standard repertoire of ecclesiastical satire in the century, but the narrator underscores the contemporaneity of his indictments with repetitions of temporis hujus and hodie. Scriptural allusions bolster the accusations that bishops are thieves, mercenaries, false prophets, and wolves; there are the familiar puns: His Lordship loves the mark (marcam) more than Mark (Marcum), lucre (lucrum) more than Luke (Lucam), the barking of hounds (canum) over canons (canones). There is even the customary play on pastor (shepherd) and pascor (I feast).[16] Amidst these conventional devices, which likely retained their appeal for Nigel's audience, if not the modern reader, a more original wit often surfaces. For example, the poet's satire of "boy bishops" is humorously enriched by diminutives and ridiculous exaggeration. "Robby" and "Willie" (Robekinus; Wileminus), wailing in their cradles and still unable to utter "Mama" and "Papa," hold the keys to the church. They are carried, in buntings and baskets, to Rome, where the deficit of their ages will be supplied by cash. This is stinging satire at its best.

The specific charges against bishops which Burnellus focuses on are their love of material goods and their neglect of spiritual offices. The shameful contrast between the ideal pastor spiritualis and the real prelate of the day is vividly illustrated in the poet's descriptions of episcopal splendor and luxury. The lavish furnishings, delicacies, fine wines of the bishop's palace (splendida tota domus) are set against empty churches and naked altars (ecclesias vacuas, altaria nuda). The bishop's passion for hunting leaves little time for sacred duties:

> If you ask what the bishop does in the city,
> He prepares to go swiftly with his hounds to the woods,
> Either to catch birds with birds, or to fish with hooks,
> And to draw in here a perch or there a pike.

A heron was spotted near the river bank;
The bishop rushes from the city to release his hawk.
He haunts forest groves more than holy places,
And he esteems dogs' barking more than Church laws.
When his hound is struck or his hawk injured, he grieves
More anxiously than if one of his clerics should die.

(Si quaeris quid agat festinus praesul in urbe,
　Assumptis canibus in nemus ire parat,
Aut ut aves avibus capiat vel piscibus hamum
　Mittat et esocem hinc trahat inde lupum.
Ardea visa fuit fluviali proxima ripae,
　Jactet ut ancipitrem praesul ab urbe ruit.
Silvarum saltus plusquam loca sancta frequentat,
　Latratusque canum canone pluris habet.
Plus cane percusso dolet anxius aut ave laesa
　Quam si decedat clericum unus ei) (2789-98)

Nigel frames such scandalous portraits with warnings of the Lord's vengeance; his sharp humor is bittersweet, and the reader clearly senses that fact. He is not surprised at the poet's passing observation that bishops of his day, when positioned before mirrors (specula), hold their eyes shut.

Though Burnellus pretends to marvel even more (magis miror) at the character of abbots and priors (2815-72), the theme is fundamentally the same as for the bishops: hypocrisy. Do not trust their words, their white garments (Ne credas verbis ne credas vestibus albis), for they are really thieves (fures). The poet signifies their deceptions by Scriptural references, e.g., they have the voice of Jacob, but the hairy bodies of Esau, and he lends immediacy to his criticisms by repetitions of nunc and hodie. Unlike the preceding section, however, this one has little humor; rather, it is pungent invective. The labels are caustic, the images beastly. Abbots and priors are like dogs who return to their own vomit (cf. Proverbs 26.11) and lap it up (sorbentque quod evomuerunt); they are like sows in mud, sly foxes in ambush; they are violent like the wolf and the horned ram; they resemble the hawk which ascends nearer to heaven that it may swoop down with greater force. The tone here is angry, the mood evident disgust, as we might expect in a monastic poet addressing the degeneracy of his superiors. Abruptly, the section ends with a declaration of fear (plura loqui timeo, ne reprehendar ego). Though Nigel's fear of censorship and recrimination may have been genuine (recall that it is expressed by Burnellus the ass), it did not prevent him from his most vehement and sustained invective in the entire Speculum Stultorum. Nevertheless, he repeats (2873-4) this concern (publicus hostis ero) as his reason for omitting laymen from his general review.

J. H. Mozley, the editor of Speculum Stultorum, pointed out that Nigel's explanatory letter to his patron contains no reference at all to the final third of the poem, suggesting that all subsequent to the review of religious orders may be a later addition.[17] This view is supported by the content, which seems far removed from the original theme. First, there is a parliament of fowls, then a tale of the three Fates of classical mythology, and, finally, an exemplum on ingratitude. Yet, Nigel clearly composed these verse narratives and incorporated them in his story of Burnellus, who remains the fundamental link between all sections of the poem.

The parliament of fowls (2875-3232) opens with the ass removing himself to a typical <u>locus amoenus</u> to meditate and write poems. He witnesses a great assembly of birds and overhears the harangues of three: the raven, cock and hawk. Their wide-ranging discourses touch briefly upon several traditional satiric themes, such as disorder in the world at large, and the debility of old age. However, the primary subject is <u>lingua loquax</u>, the folly (and danger) of imprudent babbling. The raven, whose own indiscreet chatter ruined him, still cannot repress his verbosity, though his theme is garrulousness; the cock warns of birds who imperil themselves by loose talk; the hawk, in a brief speech, denounces as the world's worst vice <u>garrula lingua</u> (babbling tongue) and <u>os pravum</u> (perverse mouth).

Surely, Nigel intended the parliament of fowls to be taken as allegory, in addition to its obvious lessons on verbal discretion. I believe that the three birds represent distinct classes in society: the raven those in religious life, the cock stands for common people, the hawk is the nobility. My view is supported by traditional lore about these birds, and internal evidence of the text. The raven had a reputation for greed, treachery and faithlessness. Medieval writers often accused religious of these vices, as in the letter of Peter the Venerable cited in chapter one. In our poem, Nigel alludes to them referring to the raven's failure to return to Noah (<u>Genesis</u> 8) because it was intent upon feeding (on cadavers!), as those in religious life abandon their monastic havens for worldly pursuits. Moreover, the passage on this bird specifically decries the loquacity of priests (<u>lingua sacerdotum</u>), and it offers a model for confessors. As the raven's address draws to a close, it observes:

And there are other birds which, for their entire lives,
Dwell in the blessed cloisters of the religious.

(Sunt et aves aliae, quae toto tempore vitae
Religiosorum claustra beata colunt) (3063-4)

The lines on the cock underscore its life of loyal service, and they warn that it could relate many horrors if its tongue were unrestrained. Specifically, it could disclose what the master (dominus) does, what the servant (servus) says, what the peasant (rusticus) whispers in his wife's ear. The hawk appeals to its own nobility in discouraging gossip and perverse speech:

We are noble, born from superior stock;
It does not befit our mouth to speak base words.

(Nos sumus ingenui, generoso stemmate nati,
Non decet os nostrum turpia verba loqui) (3203-4)

Though the assembly of birds is probably a late addition to Speculum Stultorum, its position immediately after the review of religious orders and social classes suggests that Nigel intended to link it to them, and the content seems to confirm this.

After another transitional passage in which Burnellus, meditating on the brevity of life, reaffirms his intention to enter religious life in his own new foundation, and invites Doctor Galen to join him, the ass relates an exemplum (he calls it so himself) to justify the subjection of the great to the inferior in monastic communities. He tells a tale of the Fates (the Parcae of Roman mythology) who wandered about the earth seeking to remedy the faults or defects of nature in persons (Naturae vitiis ferre salutis opem). They encounter, in turn, two lovely maidens (puella formosa; puella venusta), one weeping profusely and the other lame. The elder goddess rejects the pleas of her sisters to aid these girls on the grounds that, though they suffer an affliction, Natura has amply blessed them with beauty and nobility. She allows their abundant goods to descend only upon a peasant girl (puella rustica) who shamelessly relieves herself in their sight, for, the goddess states:

> If powerful Nature had given this wretched girl better,
> She would not have mooned us so!
>
> (Si natura potens miserae meliora dedisset,
>   Non ita monstrasset cornua luna nova.) (3403-4)

The author himself comments on the satirical thrust of this story when Burnellus affirms (3435-58) the customary practice "in religione" of advancing those who possess the fewest natural talents. This is what fosters the disasters, scandals, schisms, deceits, scorn and losses "in religione." Though all other things can be concealed, he decides, contempt for oneself (contemptum proprium) cannot. This is a defect which has no antidote.

Speculum Stultorum concludes with a long exemplum on a vexing concern of Nigel's, ingratitude. The tale is prefaced by the sudden appearance of Bernard, Burnellus' master, who seizes the wayward ass and leads him, bridled and branded, to a life of drudgery once more. This unfortunate event was foreshadowed by a nosebleed, which Burnellus recognized as a bad omen, and a string of curses invoked upon any who wished him ill. What could be a worse ill than a boorish peasant master? Burnellus' recapture by the rusticus, who is defined by such uncomplimentary adjectives as nequam (worthless), contrarius (hostile), callidus (crafty) and malignus (malicious), marks the departure of the ass from the poem, except for two passing references (3702 and 3891).

The exemplum on ingratitude, the final "inner narrative" of the poem (3561-3879), tells how Bernard rescued three wild beasts and a rich man, Dryanus, from a deep pit. He had been moved by the man's pitiful appeals and promise to divide his great wealth with his rescuer. Once safe, Dryanus denied his agreement and even threatened Bernard with harm. The beasts, however, demonstrated their gratitude. The lion brought him fresh meat, the ape gathered wood for him, the serpent presented a wondrous gem with magical properties. After popular rumor brought these remarkable events to the king's ear, he commanded Dryanus to honor his pledge, Bernard became rich, and the narrator comments on gratitude and its Scriptural commendation. The story is expanded by Nigel's exquisite sense of detail and narrative development, so that its three hundred lines are charming, never tedious.

The closing verses of Speculum Stultorum explicitly proclaim the moral of the amusing allegory which has preceded:

> The life of Burnellus becomes an example to all
> Living men, for so does the author teach.

. . . .

There are some who wish to excel at great things
And they strive toward this night and day alike.
While these seek greatness and aim toward the heights,
Often they fall suddenly, and often they fail.
To seek anything against Nature or one's lot,
No one is able to grant or to do that.
Our witness is Burnellus, who, seeking foolish ends,
Remained always what he was before.

(Cedat in exemplum cunctis viventibus ista
  Burnelli vita, nam docet auctor ita.
       . . . .
Nam sunt nonnulli transcendere magna volentes,
  Et nituntur ad hoc nocte dieque simul.
Qui dum magna petunt et semper ardua tendunt,
  Saepe repente ruunt saepeque deficiunt.
Contra naturam vel sortem quaerere quicquam,
  Nemo potest illud reddere vel facere;
Burnello teste, qui, dum quaesivit inepta,
  Semper permansit quod prius ipse fuit)

(3879-80; 3885-92)

Natural imperfections in persons, such as their lack of understanding or sensitivity, were an abiding source of frustration for Nigel of Canterbury. <u>Speculum Stultorum</u> constantly exposes the innate stupidity, greed, laziness, ingratitude of its characters, and the premise that inborn defects cannot be remedied is reiterated often in lines such as:

>Against Nature and dogs' ways to contend,
>How hard it is, no one can say.[18]
>
>(Contra naturam niti moresque caninos
> Quam sit difficile dicere nemo potest)
>   (1907-08)

The poem as a whole illustrates the thesis that no doctor, no medicine can cure the defects of nature, the <u>stigmata naturae servilis</u>, as one line (1909) has it. Thus, Burnellus must painfully discover that no one can grant what Natura denies (<u>Quod Natura negat, reddere nemo potest</u>), and the monk should learn contentment from his example. The universal precept is moderation, the reasonable cultivation and employment of one's natural talents. Nigel of Canterbury's enduring lesson is that rashness and excesses lead one inevitably to discover his own face in the "Mirror of Fools."

CHAPTER V

NOTES

[1] All textual citations of the poem are taken from the critical edition by J. H. Mozley and R. R. Raymo, Nigel de Longchamps Speculum Stultorum (Berkeley and Los Angeles, 1960). The editors briefly discuss the poem's medieval influence on pages 8-9. The entire piece was translated by J. H. Mozley, A Mirror for Fools, or the Book of Burnel the Ass (Notre Dame, Ind., 1963) and by Graydon W. Regenos, The Book of Daun Burnel the Ass: Nigellus Wireker's Speculum Stultorum (Austin, Texas, 1959).

[2] A biography was published by R. A. Beals, Nigellus Wireker (Cambridge, Ma., 1927).

[3] In his Tractatus contra Curiales et Officiales Clericos, Nigel declared that he had seen and touched Becket, eaten and drunk with him. See the edition by A. Boutemy (Paris, 1959) 151.

[4] Boutemy traces John's influence on Nigel in his introduction, pages 123-31. The Policraticus was edited by C. C. J. Webb, 2 vols. (Oxford, 1909).

[5] Jan Ziolkowski, ed. Nigel of Canterbury: Miracles of the Virgin Mary, in verse (Toronto, 1986).

[6] The letter has been published, with introduction, by J. H. Mozley, "The Epistola Ad Willelmum of Nigel Longchamps," Medium Aevum 39 (1970) 13-20.

[7] E. R. Curtius, European Literature and the Latin Middle Ages, trans. W. R. Trask (New York, 1963) 94-98.

[8] See, e.g., John's harsh words about Foliot in #292 (to the monks of Christchurch) in The Letters of John of Salisbury, Vol. Two, edited by W. J. Miller, S. J. and C. N. L. Brooke (Oxford, 1979) 666-73.

[9] The work is described by W. P. Ker, Epic and Romance (New York, 1957) 300-308.

[10] Mozley and Raymo, 6.

[11] John's theory and recent literature on it are discussed by Tilman Struve, "The Importance of the Organism in the Political Theory of John of Salisbury," in The World of John of Salisbury, ed. Michael Wilks (Oxford, 1984).

[12] Mozley and Raymo, 6.

[13] The caput mundi metaphor occurs in Walter of Chatillon's "Propter Sion non tacebo," John of Salisbury's Entheticus (1173-74) and Bernard of Morval's De contemptu mundi (3.631) among poets whom we have considered in this study. For several more instances of its use, see John A. Yunck, The Lineage of Lady Meed: The Development of Mediaeval Venality Satire (Notre Dame, 1963), chapter two, esp. 100-111.

[14] In Entheticus 1309, "Hircanus" the king is referred to as vindex ferarum (protector of wild beasts). John's Policraticus (I.4) expresses sentiments identical to Nigel's in the passage under discussion.

[15] Yunck offers many examples in ch. four, aptly entitled "Nummus vincit, Nummus regnat."

[16] Walter of Chatillon punned on the same words. See Karl Strecker's edition, page 5.

[17] J. H. Mozley, "The Epistola Ad Willelmum of Nigel of Longchamps," Medium Aevum 39 (1970) 14.

[18] Cf. lines 1125-6; 1559-60; 3419-20; 3889-90.

GENERAL BIBLIOGRAPHY ON SATIRE

Ballet-Lynn, Thérèse. Recherches sur L'Ambiguité et la Satire au Moyen Age. Paris, 1977.

Bischoff, Bernhard. "Living With the Satirists," in Classical Influences on European Culture A.D. 500-1500, edited by R. R. Bolgar. Cambridge, 1960.

Elliot, Robert C. The Power of Satire: Magic, Ritual, Art. Princeton, New Jersey, 1960.

Highet, Gilbert. Juvenal the Satirist. Oxford, 1954.

_____. The Anatomy of Satire. Princeton, New Jersey, 1962.

Hodgart, Matthew. Satire. New York, 1969.

Kernan, Alvin. The Cankered Muse. New Haven, Connecticut, 1976 repr.

Lehmann, Paul. Die Parodie im Mittelalter. Stuttgart, 1963 repr.

Mack, Maynard. "The Muse of Satire," The Yale Review XLI (1951) 80-92.

Mann, Jill. "Satiric Subject and Satiric Object in Goliardic Literature," Mittellateinisches Jahrbuch 15 (1980) 63-86.

Paulson, Ronald, ed. Satire: Modern Essays in Criticism. Englewood Cliffs, New Jersey, 1971.

Peter, John. Complaint and Satire in Early English Literature. Oxford, 1956.

Raby, F. J. E. <u>A History of Secular Latin Poetry in the Middle Ages</u>. 2 vols. Oxford, 1934.

Rawson, Claude, ed. <u>English Satire and the Satiric Tradition</u>. Oxford, 1984.

Rigg, A. G. "Golias and Other Pseudonyms," <u>Studi Medievali</u> Series 3, number 18 (January, 1977) 65-109.

Schüppert, Helga. <u>Kirchenkritik in der lateinischen Lyrik des 12. und 13. Jahrhunderts</u>. Munich, 1972.

Thomson, Rodney M. "The Origins of Latin Satire in Twelfth Century Europe," <u>Mittellateinisches Jahrbuch</u> 13 (1977) 73-83.

Weston, Arthur. <u>Latin Satirical Writing Subsequent to Juvenal</u>. Lancaster, Pennsylvania, 1915.

Wiesen, David S. <u>St. Jerome as a Satirist</u>. Ithaca, New York, 1964.

Witke, Charles. <u>Latin Satire: The Structure of Persuasion</u>. Leiden, 1970.

Wright, Thomas, ed. <u>Anglo-Latin Satirical Poets and Epigrammatists of the XIIth Century</u>. 2 vols. London, 1872.

Yunck, John A. <u>The Lineage of Lady Meed: The Development of Mediaeval Venality Satire</u>. South Bend, Indiana, 1963.

INDEX

Aaron, 56-57
Abelard, 80
Absalom, 45
Adam, 17, 33, 49-50, 52
Adversus Jovinianum, 12, 17
Aeneid, 35, 83
Alan of Lille, 34, 100
Alberic, 80, 88
Alecto, 101, 103, 109
Alexander III (Pope), 96, 100
Alexandreis, 91, 96
Amiens, 80, 91
Ammon (Jupiter), 50-51
Amphiaraus, 13
Anselm of Canterbury, 34
Antichrist, 34-35, 101-111
Apocalypse, 42
Apocolocyntosis, 3
Apollo, 17
Apology (St. Bernard), 22
Apulia, 132
Architrenius, 10
"Archpoet," 19
"Archpoet's Confession," 19
"Arnold," 131-134
Ars Amatoria, 3, 36, 44, 98
Ars Poetica, 33
Augustine, (St.), 43
"Aureolus," 17-18, 20
Austin Canons, 143, 146

Babylon, 47-48
Bacchus, 134
Bakelfest, 95, 101
Bataille des Sept Arts, 77
Beauvais, 78
Becket, Thomas, 91, 105, 112, 126
Beelzebub, 103, 108, 112
"Bernard," 154-155
Bernard of Clairvaux, 7, 22, 32, 34
Bernard of Morval, 5-6, 14, 18, 24, 31-64; passim, 83, 144, 147
Bernardus Silvestris, 100
Besancon, 101

"Bicornis," 122-124
Boethius, 70, 100
Bologna, 91, 131
"Boy bishops," 5-6, 54, 139-140
Briareus, 82-83
"Brunetta," 122-124
Burnellus, 24, 117-159 passim

Calixtus III (anti-Pope), 96, 100
Canterbury, 118, 124, 126
Canterbury Tales, 117, 143
Carmina Burana, 5
Carthusians, 8, 146
Cathedral schools, 1-2
Cato, 39, 44, 120
Cena Trimalchionis, 3
Cerberus, 112
Charybdis, 94
Chaucer, Geoffrey, 6, 18, 47, 117, 132, 140, 143
Chytraeus, Nathan, 31
Cicero, 42-44, 98, 120
Cistercians, 7-8, 127-129, 143-146
Cluny (Cluniacs), 8, 22-24, 32, 58, 143, 146, 148
Conrad of Hirsau, 34
"Coppa," 132
"Cornificius," 9, 92
"Crassus," 94
Cynyras, 13

"Dacianus," 83
Damian, Peter, 59
Dante, 35, 44
Darius, 96
David, 15-18, 20, 50, 52
"De contemptu mundi," 5, 18, 31-64; passim, 83
"De miseria conditionis humanae," 34
Democritus, 41
"De muliere mala," 13
De nugis curialium, 7, 18
Deuteronomy, 43
"De vita monachorum," 6
Dialogus de mundi contemptu vel amore, 34
Dido, 43
Diogenas, 41, 92
Diomedes, 40
Disticha Catonis, 44
"Dryanus," 155-156

Eco, Umberto, 117
Eden, 46
Elias, 106, 111

Ennius, 2
Enoch 106, 111
Entheticus, 9-10, 19, 118, 131, 148
Epicurus, 55, 57
Esau, 85, 151
Eunuchus, 74, 80
Eurydice, 75
Eve, 33
Exodus, 43

Fates, 139, 151, 153
"Flora," 68-73
Foliot, Gilbert, 7, 125
Frederick I, 96, 105, 110, 112
"Fromund," 128-130
Fulgentius, 100
Furies, 101, 107, 112

Galen of Pergamum, 121
Ganymede, 45, 109
"Gargantua," 142
Garin de Loherain, 130
Genesis, 152
Gerald of Wales, 7, 142
Giezi, 5, 93, 105, 110, 112
Gilbertines, 145-146
Gnatho, 80
Golden Age, 36-38, 46
"Goliards," 19, 98
Gomorrha, 45
Gower, John, 117
Grandmontines, 143-146
Gregorian reforms, 2
Gregory I (Pope), 42-43
"Gundulf," 132

Haskins, C.H., 1
Hector, 45
Hell, 11-12, 35, 45
Henri d'Andeli, 67
Henry II, 91
Henry of Huntingdon, 18, 34, 47
Hercules, 17
Heroides, 44
Hexameter, 3, 59, 73, 81, 98
Hildebert of Lavardin, 13-15, 49, 59
Hippolytus, 13, 15, 45, 49-51
"Hircanus," 10
Historia Anglorum, 18
Homer, 75, 92
Homosexuality, 53, 76

Horace, 3-4, 33, 39-40, 46, 67-68, 75, 84, 90, 97-98, 119, 144
"Hora Novissima," 32
Hospitallers, 8, 143-146
Hoskier, H.C., 60
Hugh of Orleans, 23, 65-88 passim

Inferno, 35
Innocent III (Pope), 34
Isaiah, 147

Jackson, S.M., 52, 58
Jacob, 85, 151
Jerome, St., 4, 12-13, 16-18, 20, 41-43, 52-53
Jesuits, 32
Jesus, 35
Job, 42, 139
John de Hauville, 10
John of Salisbury, 4, 6-10, 19-21, 67, 90, 92, 98, 118, 126, 131, 142-144, 148
John the Baptist, 13-15, 49-51
John the Evangelist, 34, 80
Joseph, 13-15, 45, 49-51
Jovinian, 13, 17
Judas, 81, 83, 148
Juno, 45
Jupiter, 17
Juvenal, 3-4, 12, 20, 38-41, 42, 46, 49, 53, 76, 90, 93, 98

Kernan, Alvin, 66
Knights Templar, 8, 143-146

La Commedia, 44
Laon, 90
Lateran Council (1179), 5
Lazarus, 83
Leah, 106, 111-112
Lille, 90
Locusta, 48
London, 125-126
Lot, 16
Lotario Dei Segni (Innocent III), 34
Lubin, Eilhard, 32
Lucan, 1, 44, 98
Lucilius, 2, 39, 67
Luke, St., 82-83, 149
Lyon, 128

Macrobius, 100
Map, Walter, 7-8, 11-12, 17-18, 129, 142
Marbod of Rennes, 13-14, 49
Marcus Aurelius, 121
"Mariale," 32

Mark, St., 149
Mars, 17
Martial, 3
Martianus Capella, 80, 100
Matthew of Vendome, 67
Matthew, St., 120
<u>Medea</u>, 17
Menippean satire, 89
<u>Metalogicon</u>, 8
<u>Metamorphoses</u>, 44
"Metamorphosis Goliae," 19
Misogamy, 12-13, 16-17
Misogyny, 3, 12-16, 20, 48, 76
Moses, 95
Mozley, J.H., 151
"Mundus Deciduus," 34

<u>Name of the Rose</u>, 117
Nature (<u>Natura</u>), 10, 121, 135-136, 154, 157
Neale, J.M., 32
Neckam, Alexander, 67
Nero, 104, 109, 112
Nestor, 147
Nigel of Canterbury, 5-6, 8, 10, 18-19, 24, 47, 117-159 <u>passim</u>
"Nightingale and Thrush," 16
Nisus, 13
Noah, 152
Normandy, 118
Nuns, 144-146
"Nun's Priests's Tale," 132

Odyssey, 75
<u>Ordo Monasticus</u>, 6
Orpheus, 75
Ovid, 3, 17, 36-37, 44, 46, 98, 112
Owst, G.R., 20

Parcae, 144
Parker, Horatio, 32
Paris, 10, 15, 82, 90, 134, 139-142
Parody, 4, 83, 123, 130
Paschal III (anti-Pope), 96
Paul, St., 112
"Pecunia," 37
Penelope, 76-77
<u>Peristephanon</u>, 83
Persius, 3, 39, 98
Peter of Blois, 20-23
Peter the Venerable, 22, 31-33, 58-59, 152
Petronilla, 45
Petronius, 3

Philobiblon, 18
Pictor, Petrus, 13-15, 49
Plato, 42, 80
Pliny the Younger, 44
Pluto, 106, 112
Policraticus, 118, 143-144
Pons de Melguil, 58
Praemonstratensians, 8, 143, 146
Preble, Henry, 58
Priscian, 80
Proteus, 50-51
Proverbs, 151
Prudentius, 83
Psalms, 42, 99

Quintilian, 2

Rabelais, Francois, 142
Rachel, 106, 111-112
Reims, 70, 90
Remedia Amoris, 3, 98
Richard de Bury, 18
Richard of Poitiers, 66-67
Roger of Bec, 6
Roger of Caen, 16
Roman Curia, 5-6, 19, 91, 94, 147-148
Rome, 35, 46, 54, 75, 99, 142, 149
Ruben, 50, 52
"Ruffinus," (St.), 133
"Rufinus," 17-18

Saladin, 145
Salerno, 124-125
Salimbene, 16
Sallust, 44
Samson, 13-17, 20, 49-51
Satan, 59, 126-127
Satira communis, 18, 46-48, 146-148
Scylla, 94
Secular Canons, 144-146
Semonides, 12
Seneca, 3
Sens, 78-79
Serlo of Wilton, 67
"Sertorius," 9
Simon Magus, 5, 148
Simony, 4, 6, 37, 54, 93, 133
Sinon, 104, 109
Singula singulis, 60
Sirens, 94, 145
"Sir Gawain," 16

Sisyphus, 12
Socrates, 43, 80, 92
Sodom, 45
Solomon, 13-17, 20, 50, 52
Sophonias, 123
<u>Speculum Stultorum</u>, 5, 8, 10, 18-19, 117-159 <u>passim</u>
Suetonius, 40
Susanna, 145
Syrtes, 94

Tantalus, 11
Teiresias, 75
Terence, 3, 44, 74, 80
Tertullian, 12
Theophrastus, 17-18, 20
Thetis, 94
Thomas of Capua, 67
Tisiphone, 101, 105, 110
<u>Tractatus contra curiales</u>, 118
Trimalchio, 58
Troy, 75
"Truffator," 125-126

Ulysses, 75-76
Uriah, 15

Vagantenlieder, 83
Vagantenstrophe, 98
"Valerius," (<u>Dissuasio Valerii</u>), 17-18

Valerius Maximus, 17
Venus, 10, 19, 53
Vergil, 1, 35, 43-44, 83, 91, 98, 112, 148
Victor IV (anti-Pope), 86, 100

Walter of Chatillon, 24, 40, 89-112 <u>passim</u>
Wetherbee, Winthrop, 100
"Wife of Bath's Tale," 18
Wilchard of Lyon, 6, 59
William of Conches, 100
William of Longchamps, 119, 134
Witke, Charles, 38, 92, 99

Yunck, John, 54

Zacheus, 82-83

STUDIES IN MEDIAEVAL LITERATURE

1. J. Elizabeth Jeffrey, **Preaching At The Boundaries: Blickling Spirituality and Old English**
2. Ronald E. Pepin, **Literature of Satire in the Twelfth Century: A Neglected Mediaeval Genre**

ABP 3971

v.2